Dr. Pfeiffer's Total Nutrition

Carl C. Pfeiffer, PH.D., M.D., and Jane Banks

Simon and Schuster   *New York*

Published by Simon and Schuster
A Division of Gulf & Western Corporation
Simon & Schuster Building
Rockefeller Center
1230 Avenue of the Americas
New York, New York 10020

Designed by Irving Perkins
Manufactured in the United States of America
1   2   3   4   5   6   7   8   9   10

Library of Congress Cataloging in Publication Data

Pfeiffer, Carl Curt.
   Dr. Pfeiffer's total nutrition

   Includes index.
   1.   Minerals in human nutrition.   2.   Vitamins
in human nutrition.   3.   Cookery (Natural foods)
4.   Orthomolecular medicine.   I.   Banks, Jane,
joint author.   II.   Title.
TX553.M55P45   613.2'8   79-23597
ISBN 0-671-24059-5

☙ Contents

Introduction 9

PART ONE

1 Trace Elements: The Breakthrough That Puts
   It All Together 15
2 Taking the Mystery Out of Vitamins 26
3 Guidelines to Go By 34
4 What Diseases Menace Our Health? 37
5 What's Wrong with the Way We Eat? 45
6 How We Should Eat 54
7 There's No Trick to Weight Control 72
8 Knitting the Raveled Sleave of Care 81
9 The Alcoholic 85
10 Keeping Aging and Senility at Bay 93
11 Arthritis 99
12 Something for Everyone 103
13 Food Sources of Vitamins and Minerals 108

PART TWO : RECIPES

Soups 119
Salads 128
Seafood 134
Poultry 139
Meat 146
Vegetarian Dishes 150
Eggs 156
Vegetables 163
Breads and Such 170
Sweets 174

Index 177

Introduction

Orthomolecular means "right molecule." These right molecules are the nutrients, usually found in food but also available, thanks to our scientists, in vitamin pills. Among the essential nutrients are proteins, fats, carbohydrates, vitamins and minerals. The importance of vitamins in treating mental disorders has been known for many years. Megavitamin therapy, the use of large doses of B vitamins in particular, has been with us for more than twenty-five years. However, it remained for Dr. Carl Pfeiffer to make us aware of the importance of essential minerals in treating mental disorders. And he has been in the forefront of our great researchers and teachers in uncovering these secrets of nature, to the betterment of all mankind.

In 1968, Dr. Linus Pauling, the father of molecular biology, coined the word *orthomolecular*. He meant by this terminology that maintenance of health and treatment of disease should include the use of substances that occur naturally in the human body, such as vitamins and minerals, and that these could be adjusted to achieve optimal concentrations. This provided scientific endorsement for the use of nutrients in medical practice and took nutritional therapy a step beyond the health food store and back toward the medical practitioner's office, where it also belongs.

While there had been a handful of brilliant and courageous medical doctors using nutritional principles in their healing work, now a good many more came forward to join the Academy of Orthomolecular Psychiatry, which was founded in 1971, and the Orthomolecular Medical Society, in 1975.

Dr. Carl Pfeiffer brought to the orthomolecular movement a vast knowledge of biochemistry, particularly the importance of minerals in controlling vital reactions in the brain and nerve cells as well as in all the other cells of the body. His influence has broadened the scope of orthomolecular practice to include not only the use of vitamins and megavitamins but also the use of minerals in the treatment of psychiatric and medical disorders. In particular he has educated us to the importance of the trace elements zinc, copper and manganese in the schizophrenias. He was among the first to classify the schizophrenias according to the underlying biochemistry and thus to advance our understanding of mental disorder.

In large measure through the success of treatment methods pioneered by Dr. Pfeiffer, we know that the biochemical factors in schizophrenia can be improved and even corrected by orthomolecular means. Of course, psychological factors are also important, but our patients can often deal effectively with conflict and confusion when orthomolecular balance is restored and physical health improved.

Furthermore, the orthomolecular principles that sustain the nervous system in the face of mental distress also build up the body metabolism to cope with physical stress. Dr. Pfeiffer has prepared this compendium of his observations and advice to cover the total picture. Because of his encyclopedic knowledge of the biochemistry of health and disease and his wealth of clinical experience, many physicians will find this fascinating and informative. However, it is written simply enough for the layman. The addition of the healthful recipes of Jane Banks, well known for her previous accomplishments in *The Arthritic's Cookbook,* will no doubt make this book all the more valuable.

San Francisco
22 July 1978

RICHARD A. KUNIN, M.D.
President
California Orthomolecular
Medical Society

Part One

Part One

1 🍁 Trace Elements: The Breakthrough That Puts It All Together

We at the Brain Bio Center in Princeton, New Jersey, my clinical and research colleagues and I, can rightfully be termed the pioneers and leaders in the field of orthomolecular research. We have found that restoring our patients' nutritional balance produces remarkable results, alleviating hyperactivity, learning disabilities and senility.

What is this complicated-sounding process? Orthomolecular medicine, or biochemical treatment, is simply the correction of faulty biochemistry. The Nobel Prize–winner Linus Pauling, who coined the term *orthomolecular medicine*, defines it as the preservation of good health and the prevention and treatment of disease by varying the concentrations in the human body of the substances normally present—such as the vitamins, essential amino acids, essential fats, and minerals. In other words, *orthomolecular* simply means "right molecule," or essential nutrient, given at the right time. What a boon to discover that by adjusting diet, eliminating junk foods, adding supplements of essential vitamins, minerals, trace metals, amino acids and unsaturated oils, we can correct the chemical imbalances of disease!

15

Happily the public has been made aware of the importance of good habits of exercise, relaxation, living (it is hoped) in a clean-air community, and natural diet. We can now add to this the growing awareness of nutrition as preventive medicine; there is general agreement that the good life, the exercising of our full potential, can be enhanced most effectively by nutrient methods. Unfortunately, however, diet alone is not sufficient. I feel that the only way we can provide ourselves with a really adequate supply of these nutrients is through supplements —which of course is a refutation of most doctor's statements that, with adequate diet, supplements are unnecessary.

Perhaps the fact that till now the orthomolecular approach has been used principally in the treatment of psychiatric disorders has something to do with this. The scope is continually broadening, however, as more and more diseases and chronic problems are being successfully treated with this therapy.

The types of treatment offered by orthomolecular physicians vary, but the accent is on meganutrient therapy after careful diagnostic tests. Meganutrient therapy involves a dosage higher than the body's normal needs, such as the megavitamin therapy of niacin and vitamin C in treating schizophrenia. Through the diagnostic tests, both clinical and psychiatric, the biochemical individuality of the person can be determined and conditions ranging from heart disease and backache to loss of memory can be treated. Arthritis, for instance, which limits the use of joints, responds to zinc supplementation.

Our work at the Brain Bio Center has provided more than ample demonstration that an adequate supply of minerals, trace elements, vitamins and protein is the best insurance for keeping the body in top working order. Our major finding, perhaps, has been the importance of trace minerals. The understanding of the human body's need for trace minerals is at the exciting stage that marked the study of new vitamins in the thirties; these little-known elements can make the difference between sickness and health, often between life and death, or sanity and mental illness.

Of course the ideally balanced diet is complete in all the essential elements—true enough. However, we must face the fact, one hard for the average American to grasp, that the ideally balanced diet is nonexistent because of food processing, improper cooking and soil exhaustion. Interestingly enough, this last is probably the major culprit; the earth's soil has become depleted over the centuries. Drought, continual planting with no rotation of crops or resting periods, the natural leaching process— all these have robbed our once rich earth of many trace elements, particularly zinc. The first zinc-deficient humans were found in Iran, Iraq and Egypt, where the soil had been used continually since the beginning of history. Even here in our nation the zinc level falls below the adequate in most of the states.

All right, so what's so great about trace minerals? The very words suggest something of very little importance! Believe me, nothing could be further from the truth: trace minerals are absolutely essential for life, and your well-being is directly proportionate to the adequacy of your intake. What are they, and why do we need them?

To begin with, there are probably sixteen essential trace elements. Their biochemical role was first found in plants, then proved in animals, and now we're in the process of determining just which of these elements we need as much as the lower species do. The trace elements now known to be essential to animal and human life are copper, tin, iron, manganese, zinc, chromium, molybdenum, cobalt, vanadium, iodine, sulfur, selenium and phosphorus. In addition there are other minerals we need to sustain life, such as potassium, magnesium and calcium—one would almost think we'd be too weighted down to swim!

Actually the heavier elements such as lead, mercury and cadmium are poisons that slowly accumulate with age and become a burden to the body much like barnacles growing on a ship at sea. These poisonous heavy metals can displace the normal zinc, manganese and copper from their enzymes in brain and other body tissues; a malfunction such as hyperactivity or continuous stimulation can result. Unfortunately, even among the useful trace elements an overabundance of copper or iron can substitute for zinc, manganese and magnesium to produce a clinical manifestation of everything from arthritis to high blood pressure to insomnia. For instance, medical researchers at Georgetown University have discovered that removing zinc from the human body decreases appetite dramatically and brings about profound weight loss. "We're getting at one of the basic mechanisms of how the appetite is controlled," they say.

But let's go back to the beginning. Where did they come from, these elements? I think we all know that life started with seawater. The salts of the seawater such as magnesium, calcium, potassium and sodium mated with phosphate, chloride and carbonate to form the first cells. The role of enzymes and vitamins in incorporating the trace elements from seawater into the cells is part of the whole vast, infinitely complex network—and how marvelous to be learning how the network operates!

If we seem to speak of zinc rather frequently, it's because of its importance. Zinc has been incorporated into enzymes that are involved in some of the body's most important functions. It teams up with B_6 to transform amino and nucleic acids into what makes cells and proteins. However, the picture is complicated because zinc is antagonistic to copper—and vice versa. This means that a copper overload, from which most of us suffer, drives the zinc from our bodies. (Of this, more later.) On top of that, our food is zinc-deficient because of the depleted soil, the inadequate fertilization and the food processing. Signs of zinc deficiency range from anemia, loss of taste, acne, white spots on the fingernails, and joint pain, to insomnia and emotional problems. Anxiety, depression, irritability, may have everything to do with too much copper and not enough zinc! Foods high in zinc include oysters, herring, sunflower seeds, clams, peas and carrots, wheat bran, beef, lamb and livers. (For a more inclusive list of food sources of vitamins and minerals see Chapter 13.) However, in many cases a supplement of 15 mg of zinc gluconate is necessary.

We've found, not too incidentally, that a zinc and B_6 (pyridoxine) deficiency can mimic an iron deficiency. This doesn't sound like much until you realize what harm a supplemental excess of iron can wreak! The supplement, promoted with great fervor via television, can become an overload in the liver, lungs, pancreas and heart—and go completely unnoticed over a period of time. The only patients for whom I think iron supplements are called for are female teenagers and women during pregnancy, and even for them the iron level should be tested to determine the need. Natural sources of iron, by the way, are organ meats, wheat germ, lean meat, deep-green leafy vegetables, whole grain cereals or breads, dried fruits, legumes, shellfish and molasses. By and large, however, the general public would benefit more from additional zinc and B_6 than from additional iron.

Continuing with our list of essential elements (and we

feel it's most important that people understand what they are and what they do), we come to manganese. This one is essential to human development, to bone growth, metabolism and reproduction; it's important to many other things, maybe even mother love! Good sources of manganese are whole grain cereals such as bran, wheat, oats; corn germ; seeds and nuts, particularly walnuts; and spinach and tea leaves (of all things!).

Sulfur is a somewhat forgotten element important in many complex ways. Egg yolks are the richest source, but even the white alone is valuable; beef and the smelly foods such as onions and garlic are rich in sulfur. Every cell in our bodies contains some sulfur, particularly our skin, hair and joints.

Selenium is even more complex. We don't want to confuse the reader—but selenium in its pure form is both an essential trace mineral and one of the most poisonous minerals on earth. Properly used, it protects against the pollutant cadmium and the mercury in large fish (notably tuna and swordfish) and enhances the effectiveness of vitamin E. It is also thought to combat cancer; research has shown a direct relationship between low selenium intake and high cancer incidence; there is evidence that selenium helps ward off the onset of cancer when taken with other vitamins. Brewer's yeast, eggs, liver and garlic are rich sources of this mineral.

Do you realize that 30 percent of us are calcium deficient? Because almost all our calcium is in our bones, a deficiency naturally leads to easy fracturing; and, unfortunately, aging decreases the body's absorption of calcium. In addition, enforced bed rest or any other inactivity causes loss of calcium; exercise is one of the vital keys to retaining calcium at any age. Milk, as we all know, is the best provider of this mineral, but for those sensitive to milk (as, say, the arthritic) a supplement of dolomitic calcium and magnesium may be substituted. Cheese and bone meal are other sources, as are other minerals, the most important of these being magnesium.

Magnesium is a major trace element. Among its many tasks, it helps our enzymes catalyze chemical reactions. We have found that a high magnesium diet lowers blood pressure, and that deficiencies are found in alcoholics and people with such illnesses as cirrhosis of the liver. Processing, refining and cooking all tend to remove the magnesium from our foods; milk, nuts and whole grains are good sources for this reason. It's also found in green vegetables and seafood and can be supplemented by taking dolomite tablets.

I don't feel we can criticize the Great American Diet enough! The highly refined foods, the horrifying overuse of sugar and fats and salt, have had disastrous results, one of which is a potassium deficiency. In addition certain medications rob the body of potassium; prednisone, digitalis, water pills and ACTH all call for an extra potassium intake, as do such conditions as high blood pressure, diabetes and liver disease. Because of side effects, try to supply the extra potassium through foods rather than supplements. It ought not to be difficult to eat some of the foods rich in potassium such as wheat germ, leafy green vegetables, lentils, beans, nuts and dates and all kinds of fruit.

Molybdenum is lost to us through the refining of whole grains, but we can find it in a few foods. When one considers the alternatives to a sufficiency of this oddly named element, one is apt to pay attention. It appears to have a very beneficial effect on prevention of tooth decay; it seems to play a role in cancer of the esophagus; and it is suspected to affect the potency of older men.

Unprocessed buckwheat grain is the best food source, with lima beans running second, followed by wheat germ, oats, sunflower seeds, lentils and liver.

Chromium is the element necessary for maintaining the normal metabolism of glucose (blood sugar) and thus is involved in the newest "fashionable" disorder, functional hypoglycemia. Chromium works through the insulin hormone to effect the delicate balance between high and low blood-sugar conditions, and its best source is brewer's yeast. Other foods include liver, beef, cheese, unprocessed whole grains, dried beans, peanuts, mushrooms, beets and beer.

Cobalt is one thing of which we need very little, and it comes to us through the plants that animals feed on. Aside from its being an essential part of vitamin B_{12} no function in humans or animals is known; too much can have such an undesirable result as goiter.

Somehow, it seems as if progress always manages to exact its price! For instance, man's use of heavy metals in manufacturing greatly increased his exposure to these metals—with the expected results. Five heavy metals have been found to be intoxicants and produce, among other highly undesirable effects, mental symptoms. The toxic elements, which are those that accumulate in the tissues—mentioned previously are lead, mercury and cadmium—become with age a burden to the body.

Some patients have been diagnosed as schizophrenic when in fact they were victims of lead or mercury poisoning. A classic case in medical history is that of the felt workers known as mad hatters—owing to the mercury salts in the sizing used. Various nervous and mental disorders are traceable to lead poisoning, hyperactivity in children being one in particular. I trust children are no longer chewing on lead-based paint on their cribs!

Then we have environmental lead, thanks to the invention of the automobile. Although this pollution from auto exhaust has been substantially reduced through legislation, we still have a disturbing level of lead in our environment. Some of it comes to us through cigarette smoke, which is contaminated by the lead arsenate applied to tobacco as an insecticide (another reason for giving us a choice of whether to breathe cigarette smoke or not!). We ingest lead in drinking water that travels through lead pipes (possibly we get even more from brass-activated carbon filters), and inhale fumes of it from lead-based paint. (There has been speculation that the mental illness that changed Goya's entire creative expression as a painter was the result of years of use of lead-based paint.)

Mercury, another extremely harmful heavy metal, comes to us in the form of pesticides. It is hoped, however, that through legislation we will eventually manage to control this threat to our health. A second major source of mercury is large fish; the mercury released into the waters of the world through industry reaches the fish through their food, mainly algae. The larger the fish, the more poison it retains, thus making large fish like swordfish and tuna highly suspect unless one is certain of the waters whence they came.

Sources of the heavy metal cadmium include, again, water from pipes that may contain cadmium (owing to long-ago galvanizing processes), and tobacco smoke. In addition, coal burning and excessive use of refined foods produce cadmium—this last because of the lack of zinc in refined foods, cadmium being antagonistic to zinc. Unfortunately, cadmium can replace zinc in the body and cause high blood pressure and other cardiovascular diseases; excess cadmium can increase the sense of pain. As if that weren't enough, recent statistical evidence has led some doctors to suggest that *excesses* of cadmium or copper, or *deficiencies* of zinc, vanadium or chrome may be critical factors in death from heart attacks.

Bismuth, a heavy metal with no natural function as far as is known, is another metal found to produce mental disorders. We've found that the use of bismuth salts or other preparations containing bismuth such as rectal suppositories can produce an intoxication resembling mental illness. Repeated oral use of bismuth in any form is certainly to be avoided like the plague.

And now finally we have the fifth heavy-metal intoxicant, copper. To put it simply, it's just that there's too much copper around! Anyone who eats and drinks gets copper! Found in all iron salts, it *is* an element necessary for the manufacture of hemoglobin. However, it is highly unlikely that a copper deficiency can occur in man, as we are quite literally deluged with copper through sources such as our water, cigarette smoke, automobile pollution, birth control pills and multiple vitamins containing copper. Even our cooking utensils made beautiful with copper add to the insult! And on top of all this we know that copper has a tendency to accumulate in the blood.

Conditions affected by a high level of copper in the body range from hypertension and heart attacks to schizophrenia, migraine headaches and senility. Fortunately, as mentioned earlier, zinc is antagonistic to copper, so we have a remedy for the excess copper condition. The solution is simply to supplement the zinc and thus control the copper. Restoration of this vitally important mineral balance can combat some of mankind's most common scourges. There's even strong evidence that correction of chronic zinc and B_6 deficiency may avoid a predisposition of cells to cancer.

All this may be somewhat confusing to the layman,

but believe me, it's worth taking a good look at the part these elements play in the operation of that body of yours! After all, it's the only one you've got, and the quality of your life definitely depends on the care you give that body.

2 🍁 Taking the Mystery Out of Vitamins

Anyone who has recently gone into any health food store understands this chapter heading! Shelves loaded with bottles of vitamins and minerals; many labels, widely varying prices for the same item, dosages in mg and mcgm and grm, no one to help you except perhaps a young clerk who wants to make the biggest possible sale. Fifteen minutes later you leave with a heavy bag of bottles and an empty billfold, still in the dark as to the what, why and when of these things you're pretty sure you need.

Before purchasing, the consumer should be familiar with what has or has not been proved concerning the effectiveness of any product; all of us talk a lot about vitamins without really knowing much about what they are and why they're so important. What *are* they? What *is* adequate protection?

The *RDA* (for Recommended Daily Allowance), a government publication first published in 1943, is the best source of complete vitamin information. (Don't confuse it with the *USRD*, which is concerned with the labeling on a product.) The vitamins we know most about are vitamin A (carotene), vitamin B_1 (thiamin), B_2 (riboflavin), B_6 (pyridoxine), the other members of the vitamin B complex (biotin, folic acid, choline, niacin, inositol, pantothenic acid, para-aminobenzoic acid), vitamin C (ascorbic acid), vitamin D (calciferol and 7-dehydrocholesterol), vitamin E (tocopherol), vitamins F, K, L_1, L_2, M and P.

Ideally, of course, the proper balance of these chemicals would be present in our food; this is quite out of the question for the same reasons as stated in the previous chapter—soil depletion, food processing and improper cooking. Many doctors deride the need for additional vitamins in the form of supplements; this attitude, however, is gradually changing. As Dr. Dorothy G. Weible of the Milbank Memorial Fund said: "The reason that nutritional deficiencies are allowed to go unchecked and unnoticed is that doctors don't know how to test for such deficiencies."

We create our own deficiencies, or the environment creates them for us. For example, cigarettes destroy a large amount of vitamin C. Alcohol and artificial sweets rob us of B vitamins, and chemicals used in food processing do the same. Add to these such poisons in our environment as carbon monoxide and we must certainly realize we must take extra vitamins—especially B and C, which aid in the excretion of poisons from the body. We destroy vitamins and minerals in our kitchens as we peel and sometimes unnecessarily wash and cook. Also, every year of a person's life brings additional nutritional needs. The aging process creates its own demands; extra vitamins can prevent senility and probably help us keep our sight and hearing.

Furthermore, how practical is it for most people to manage a perfectly balanced diet? In our kitchens we can at least try, but some of us must depend on restaurants. The latter can at least select the most beneficial foods from a menu (in the back of the book you'll find a list of the foods richest in the various minerals and vitamins). However, going on the assumption—and I'm afraid we must—that your diet is not going to provide you with all the nutritional protection you need, we've outlined what we consider proper nutrition therapy.

Vitamin A is one of the few vitamins that can become toxic in overdosage. However, our foods supply us with a fairly generous amount: the egg is rich in it, and milk and margarine have been enriched with it. The latter, incidentally, contains thirteen times the vitamin A as does butter. A supplement of 25,000 IU (international units) a day is suggested to help the skin and possibly prevent cancer of the surfaces and linings of tissues. This daily dosage is not excessive, but too much can cause skin peeling, headaches and increased intracranial pressure. Vitamin A in conjunction with B_6, B_2, zinc and vitamin E has been helpful in relieving acne and excessively oily skin.

We recommend as a supplement to the appropriate food an adequate intake of the B vitamins together (B complex). Super-B-50, or a comparable one, is good; avoid multivitamins "with minerals" because of the copper content. This balance of the B vitamins will give you thiamine; riboflavin (which will color the urine a deep yellow—not to worry!); niacin, which along with its other benefits has been found to be extremely helpful in the treatment of arthritis and the regulation of blood cholesterol; pyridoxine, which along with zinc is lost from the body during stress and will perhaps not be adequate in the one multivitamin (one or two 50-mg tablets of B_6 may be added to produce pleasant dream recall, a normal guide). The B_{12} present in multivitamins is almost useless because B_{12} is not absorbed well by the intestines and must be given by injection. There will probably be other elements present such as folic acid and calcium; check these carefully to be sure you don't double-dose yourself. Actually, most excesses are excreted harmlessly, but A, D, K and folic acid should not be taken beyond the prescribed allowance.

A substitute (or addition to, if the need dictates) for the above capsule is at least six tablets of brewer's yeast; brewer's yeast contains most of the B vitamins in a natural form as well as the chromium-containing vitamin called the "glucose tolerance factor," which may prevent adult diabetes. Selenium, which protects against the toxic effects of the pollutant cadmium and the high mercury in fish, is also present; selenium also appears to reduce the chances of all types of cancer. It's advisable to start with two brewer's yeast tablets and raise the dosage gradually, since the yeast may initially cause intestinal gas owing to flora changes in the gut.

Then—and it's a big then—we come to the useful vitamin C, or ascorbic acid. Whether or not it cures the common cold as claimed by the brilliant Linus Pauling (and it certainly seems to), vitamin C is known to be essential for many biochemical functions; it acts rather like the gears for the rest of the vitamins. Vitamin C is an essential food substance. Man does not synthesize it in his body, nor does he store it for long; it must be ingested frequently.

C controls the ability of the body to produce collagen, which is intercellular material; the dentine of teeth, the bones and connective tissues also depend on it. In addition, C has recently been found to have an antianxiety effect. It also mobilizes heavy metals such as copper, lead and mercury, allowing their excretion by the kidneys; this excretion is greater when combined with zinc. People who smoke and women on the pill are among those who require a larger intake of C. Five hundred to 1,000 mg a day is an average adult dosage, but this amount should be divided into two or three dosages during a 24-hour period because C has a life of about six hours in the body.

Incidentally, one can test oneself for adequate intake of C. A dipstick, made for this purpose, can be purchased at the pharmacy. The urine can be tested with this for spill-out of C; if there is no spill-out the C should be increased. As a very general run one might start, for measuring purposes, with 500 mg morning and night.

Evidence mounts that vitamin C is effective against many diseases. Studies by Dr. Ewan Cameron, chief surgeon of Vale of Leven Hospital, Loch Lomondside, Scotland, has treated advanced cancer patients with large amounts of vitamin C with impressive results. A striking majority of these terminal cancer patients lived four years longer than expected.

The general idea is that vitamin C in large doses potentiates the natural protective mechanisms of the body so that they provide a significant amount of protection against various diseases. Much more needs to be learned about the mechanisms of the action of vitamin C against infectious and degenerative diseases; this important research is currently being carried on at the Linus Pauling Institute of Science and Medicine. One would hope that the National Cancer Foundation would follow up on whether this harmless vitamin might be effective in the fight against this hideous scourge of the world.

In addition to the strong indications that C is effective against the common cold, there are other conditions it affects favorably. Recent studies have shown vitamin C to be necessary for cholesterol regulation. The arthritic requires more than the normal amount of C to remove the heavy burden of iron and copper in the joints. It is also being used in the treatment of schizophrenia and serum hepatitis as well.

Foods highest in vitamin C are citrus fruits, green peppers, tomatoes and such green vegetables as broccoli and brussels sprouts. Because it is unlikely that any of us eat enough of these to supply our needs for normal functioning, a supplement is almost universally necessary. The purist may insist that natural rose-hip vitamin C is superior to the synthetic product, but it is five to ten times as expensive as the synthetic. Of course such natural sources as oranges are better because they provide other benefits as well, but for the average person the vitamin C that is synthetic ascorbic acid will serve the purpose.

We need not concern ourselves unduly with vitamin D, as we get a good supply from milk, fish and egg yolks. However, those whose life keeps them cooped indoors might take fish liver oil, paying close attention to the recommended dosage on the bottle because in overdose this is a vitamin toxic.

The early work in the chemical substance known as vitamin E (tocopherol) was mistakenly involved with the treatment of sterility. E affects the reproductive mechanism of laboratory animals but so far has not been found useful in the treatment of humans in this respect. On the other hand, the current vital role of vitamin E is that of an antioxidant. An antioxidant is a substance that, when combined with oxygen, shields other chemicals from the exposure to oxygen. It inhibits the destruction or modification of other chemicals. It also apparently combines with oxygen to keep blood-destroying agents from the red blood cells.

Vitamin E is helpful in treating and preventing most heart and skin diseases and also is recommended, in combination with dolomite tablets, for preventing nighttime leg cramps. E is a stimulant to the brain, so it makes sense to take the daily dose of at least 400 IU in the morning. The dosage should be increased gradually, if needed, as a sharp increase may raise the blood pressure temporarily. Its antioxidant quality may help prevent aging—many feel the oil is of benefit to the aging skin—but this may be wishful thinking. One can always try, however! In any event, vitamin E is an important asset.

Among the lesser-known vitamins is a group that are water soluble. Among them is inositol, which has a relaxing effect similar to that of Valium. Another, deaner, is the vitamin choline with one methyl group removed. As such, the deaner goes to the brain more easily than choline to build acetylcholine, the working transmitter of the brain. Deaner occurs naturally in fishy foods. A third water-soluble, folic acid, is one that can be obtained only on prescription, because excessive doses may be dangerous. In some women oral contraceptives have produced a deficiency of folic acid; it has also been used in the regulation of serum cholesterol. In conjunction with 1-mg injections of B_{12} it has been useful in the correction of anemia.

B_{12} is the one vitamin that must be injected because, as we have indicated, it is not absorbed well through the intestines. This should pose no problem—one can hardly feel the tiny disposable needle. A once-a-week shot of B_{12} has been found to be beneficial for many individuals who don't necessarily display signs of deficiency; it relieves muscle fatigue and supplies extra energy. The improvement in a feeling of general well-being makes it well worth the effort; injections of B_{12} cause no local reactions and it is nontoxic. This too requires a prescription, and some internists refuse B_{12} to their patients on the ground that it is necessary only for the treatment of pernicious anemia. The wise use of B_{12} injections with folic acid has helped many, many exhausted people!

3 🍁 Guidelines to Go By

It goes without saying that we all recognize the need for vitamins and minerals. And we're probably all in agreement that supplying these needs through our diet is preferable but well nigh impossible. What then? Self-diagnosis, except concerning the most basic needs, is very unwise; as we've mentioned, some substances can become toxic, even dangerously so, in overdosage.

The prime purpose of this book is to educate the reader so that he can educate his doctor. Our requirements for minerals and vitamins are as individual as our fingerprints; each person must discover the minimum daily requirements of his or her particular body chemistry.

The reader should encourage his general practitioner to have him tested by such means as blood, hair and nail samples. There are more and more laboratories available to do this testing, as the public is becoming more educated to the need for them. A complete biochemical analysis such as that done at the Brain Bio Center may not always be available, although most big cities now have such facilities as well as doctors who are glad to use them. The levels of copper, zinc, iron and lead in the blood should be tested, as well as such other clues to health as glucose, uric acid and cholesterol.

The doctor should also be asking questions—questions concerning dream recall, alcohol tolerance, sense of taste, memory. For instance, depression and anxiety revealed by these questions could be stemming from a copper toxicity; copper toxicity can lead to large scale psychosis, even paranoia. Is the doctor alert to such signals as thought disorder, stuttering, headaches, metallic taste, low blood histamine? Is the doctor *interested* in your biochemistry?

Even though almost all of us are zinc-deficient, it is unlikely that the general practitioner will take this into account unless talked into doing so. When he starts looking for white spots on the nails, when he starts linking anemia and insomnia, acne and joint pain, hair loss and emotional problems to a zinc-copper imbalance, we'll be getting someplace. How tragic that these conditions can exist in spite of the simplicity and ease of both the testing and the therapy!

The evidence that nutrition plays a role in almost all diseases is mounting daily. An increasing number of scientists and physicians are concluding that nutritional deficiencies can trigger behavior leading to violent, even criminal, acts. For instance, in some cases hypoglycemia (of which more in the next chapter) can set off irrational behavior that can be controlled through the diet. Although the disease involves a lower-than-normal level of sugar in the blood the treatment is to replace sweets and starches with high protein foods, fresh fruits and vegetables and vitamin and mineral supplements.

Dr. Yukio Tanaka of St. Mary's Hospital in Montreal has made studies that show that a shortage of manganese may be the cause of convulsions and epilepsy. Dr. Peter Simkin of the University of Washington has successfully treated arthritic patients with zinc sulfate; doctors don't know why, but people with rheumatoid arthritis lack zinc. Other examples of a definite relationship between mineral and vitamin deficiency and disease abound.

Therefore, proper mineral and vitamin supplementation has to be the most important facet of preventive medicine. How to determine the needs? The best way, as mentioned earlier, is to have a cooperative, forward-looking doctor. The proper testing is the surest way to determine the exact needs.

However, in spite of individual differences, there are certain nutriments which can be safely recommended to everyone. Excesses are harmlessly excreted in all but a few instances—such as the aforementioned vitamins A and D, which can be toxic in overdose.

In the back of the book is a list of supplements we consider essential, with trade names where necessary. In general, the daily intake should include a multivitamin with no copper or iron, from 200 to 400 IU of vitamin E, 15 mg of zinc gluconate morning and night plus 50 mg of B_6 morning and night. The need for C is so very personalized, but can be tested with the dipstick as suggested after starting on 500 mg. And don't forget that brewer's yeast supplies vitamins and minerals in a natural form, particularly an organic form of chromium.

The Brain Bio Center also uses a psychiatric rating test called the "Experiential World Inventory." The test, which was devised by Drs. Osmond and El-Meligi, discloses disperceptions, which are defined as abnormal viewing of the world and its people. My colleagues and I feel this test should be standard in all schools and other institutions where our young people are evaluated. The test is available from Mens Sana Publishing Inc., P.O. Box 2966, Grand Central Station, New York, N.Y. 10017.

4 🍁 What Diseases Menace Our Health?

The AMA lists our most serious public health menaces as heart disease, cancer, mental illness and alcoholism. The first definitely responds, as we will show, to mineral and vitamin therapy. There are now indications the second does also, and our work at the Brain Bio Center most definitely proves the case for the third. The fourth, alcoholism, is taken up in a later chapter.

And what of all the hidden poisons we're subjected to? Cadmium-polluted air, water and food contribute to high blood pressure and hardening of the arteries; asbestos fiber can cause lung cancer; gas cooking stoves pollute the air; fluorescent lighting can cause hyperactivity; aluminum-sulphate-clarified drinking water causes aluminum poisoning; copper plumbing can result in many disorders including hypertension; high sugar intake contributes to hypoglycemia and diabetes; food additives can afflict our children with allergies. We *must* become more aware of our dangerously polluted environment and nutrient-stripped, refined foods. Thus orthomolecular therapy is both preventive and corrective.

Because orthomolecular treatments often take months to show major results, the crisis-oriented doctor is not

37

likely to use meganutrients to treat pain, insomnia, headaches or depression. Orthodox treatment for these symptoms is usually with pain killers, sleeping pills or psychotherapy—all of which may be effective but are seldom curative. Although it is becoming common knowledge that orthomolecular medicine corrects biochemical imbalances, it's little known that in certain combinations meganutrients can be as immediately effective as a potent pain killer or tranquilizer. Niacin and vitamin C in mild doses can provide almost instant relief to the overactive mind; they can help focus mental concentration. Pyridoxine with zinc and manganese is particularly effective in relieving the symptoms of hypoglycemia. These treatments have no long-term or immediate adverse effects, while aspirin may eat away your stomach lining, and tranquilizers can cause, among other things, a grotesque shaking condition that mimics Parkinson's disease. So—meganutrients treat both the immediate and long-range causes of diseases rooted in our past dietary and physical indiscretions. There is no justification for the use of drugs except in the case of the critically ill. Generally the use of drugs is a self-deception that sacrifices long-term health for immediate relief.

Let's look first at heart attacks and angina. One of nutrition's most important roles is supplying the *proper* nutrients to the heart. For instance, we know that heart victims show an increased level of copper, and that copper raises blood pressure. We also know that zinc counteracts copper—ergo, zinc, along with B_6 and C and other minerals and vitamins, is good preventive medicine against heart attacks and strokes. The copper-contaminated water from our pipes may be a contributing factor; the solution is to "run water to waste before you taste" or to buy bottled water for drinking.

When it comes to diet, suffice it to say that the average

diet does not contain the potassium, magnesium, manganese, calcium, zinc, sulfur, selenium and phosphate needed by the beating heart! Ideally, these minerals would be supplied by natural foods such as fresh fruits and vegetables, grains and eggs, and the addition of some supplements. Potassium and magnesium are probably the hardest to come by in sufficient quantities, and when you understand that the diuretics (water pill) that many heart patients take deplete the body of both these chemicals, you realize the problem. These chemicals, along with zinc and manganese, are also stripped from the diet by processing and refining. We recommend Morton's Salt Substitute, high in potassium, for all heart patients, plus a milk of magnesia tablet 4 times a day.

Zinc—up to 30 mgm of zinc gluconate morning and night—is helpful in keeping down the cholesterol. And 200 to 400 IU of vitamin E may allay such symptoms as irregular pulse, ankle swelling and chest pain. A week-on, week-off trial is suggested to test whether or not it is helpful. Vitamin A is another vitamin needed by the heart in adequate dosage. We recommend 25,000 IU daily to promote the regulation of beats. Inositol is a relaxing vitamin and can take the place of Valium. Two tablets of 650 mgm morning and evening lowers elevated blood pressure and thus is helpful to hypertensives with heart disease.

This last, hypertension, is probably the number one threat to American health. It's a good example, however, of an illness that can be controlled with vitamin-mineral therapy. Hypertensives have been found, almost without exception, to be high in copper and low in zinc. In addition to requiring zinc supplements the hypertensive needs additional B_6, plenty of C and E and 1 gm of inositol night and morning. This last produces sedation and a gradual lowering of blood pressure. Also, studies at the

Brain Bio Center have shown that a high magnesium diet lowers blood pressure; yet, as we've said, we're apt to become deficient in it.

Exercise—good, vigorous exercise to tolerance that steps up the heartbeat to maximum and leaves the exerciser fatigued and breathless—is the other absolute must for the heart patient. As a matter of fact, exercise is an absolute must for all of us. No matter what the problem, when meganutrients are not entirely effective, good exercise to the limits of tolerance will almost always complete the cure. Jogging, bicycling, manual labor—it matters not, as long as it's vigorous and *daily*. A memorized routine of well-planned exercises done to a record, say, by the Tijuana Brass, every morning on rising, is completely adequate as long as the exercises are strenuous enough to make the heart race, the circulation flush the face and the breath come in deep gasps.

Cancer, as we've mentioned, has had some encouraging remissions with the use of vitamin C. As for mental illness, my clinical reputation has been built on work in schizophrenia. When you realize that one out of every ten Americans suffers from some form of mental or emotional disturbance, you can comprehend the importance of dealing with these problems.

It would be impossible to detail in this limited space the six differentiations of schizophrenia. On the other hand, we can point out symptoms the doctor should look for, such as low histamine in blood testing.

Most people think of histamine only in terms of "antihistamine." Actually, histamine is an important transmitter of nerve impulses throughout the body and to the part of the brain which regulates emotions and behavior. This area of the brain is loaded with zinc, which is needed to store histamine in the terminal buds of the mossy fibers. These terminal buds will release histamine to cause nerve impulses that regulate behavior. Adequate zinc and histamine equals normal behavior, while inadequate zinc and histamine equals paranoia, hallucinations and a myriad of other undesirables.

Schizophrenics are found to be very high in copper; zinc plus manganese can provide for the excretion of copper. Modern studies have found serum copper elevation in some manic-depressives, epileptics, alcoholics and victims of infectious diseases and cancer. It's interesting to note that any biological state that brings on high copper increases the body's need for vitamin C.

Food allergies can play a very large part in mental disturbances. There is the allergic child, suffering from the so-called allergic-tension-fatigue syndrome, who manifests his disturbance with irritability, hyperactivity and impaired concentration. The most commonly implicated foods are milk, wheat, beef, egg, corn, cane sugar and chocolate. In adults the condition is called cerebral allergy, in which a hidden sensitivity to one's daily bread may well be the cause of compulsive and ritualistic behavior, impaired speech development, and mood and behavior changes.

Perhaps our most important breakthrough has been the discovery of the use of pyridoxine and zinc. This deficiency leads to one form of schizophrenia in particular, pyroluria. At the Brain Bio Center this is called the "Sara Syndrome" because it was during the treatment of her dramatic case in 1971 that we discovered the miracle of zinc and B_6 (pyridoxine). In 1973 we discovered that B_6 supplementation produces dreams and dream recall, which are normal in a healthy individual.

Running close behind the above conditions is functional hypoglycemia. Functional hypoglycemia *per se* is not a disease; the term has become synonymous with chronic low blood sugar resulting from some error in body regulation of blood glucose levels. This regulation is too complex for the layman to understand, but it involves the hormone insulin and the pituitary and the adrenal glands. We know, however, that many vitamins and trace elements—such as vitamin C, the B complex vitamins, calcium, potassium, magnesium, zinc and phosphorus—mediate the glucose metabolism and control the activities of the endocrine glands. If the delicate balance of these activities is disturbed the result is chronic low blood sugar.

Of all the organs and tissues in the body, the central nervous system is the most dependent on the minute-by-minute supply of glucose from the blood. When the blood-sugar level drops, the brain immediately suffers the effects. This condition is becoming increasingly noted and has had correspondingly increasing attention from scientists and physicians of late.

Functional hypoglycemia symptoms develop in response to food intake, and the symptoms run from those "late afternoon blues," the need for a short nap or a quick snack to revive sinking spirits, to physical and emotional disturbances. Undiagnosed and untreated, the condition can lead to diabetes—which as we know can in turn lead to blindness. Why is this condition so with us now?

The sharply rising incidence of functional hypoglycemia in modern times is probably due to the greatly increased consumption of refined sugar in the past fifty to one hundred years. In the nineteenth century the per capita intake of sugar was measured in England and found to be only seven pounds per person per year. Today, people in the Western countries consume 128 pounds of sugar each year! Mark Twain once advised that "the secret to success in life is to eat what you like and let the food fight it out inside," but this statement was made long before anyone dreamed of the kinds of foods on the market shelves today. The food is indeed "fighting it out inside" and in too many cases wholly defeating the glucose regulatory mechanisms. It's estimated that at least ten million people in the United States today suffer from functional hypoglycemia.

What to do about it? Obviously, sugar intake must be drastically reduced, if not completely eliminated. The diet must be strictly adhered to. It should be high in protein, moderate in fat and low in carbohydrate. It should include not a drop of alcohol, coffee or tea and no tobacco. Instead of the traditional three-meals-a-day pattern, frequent small meals are recommended to provide a continuous source of nourishment that won't raise blood sugar. To ensure a supply of essential nutrients there must be vitamin and mineral supplements such as B complex and vitamins A and C. Manganese is needed, as well as choline, zinc and chromium. The functional hypoglycemia patient is urged to engage in increasingly active daily exercise; patients on regular exercise programs find severe symptoms very much benefited.

Pollution, though it's not in the AMA's list, is another ever-present health hazard. We're surrounded, we're assaulted by environmental poisons, but there are means of protecting ourselves. Vitamin C is the number one antitoxin; it protects the vital organs and glands and minimizes poisoning. Vitamin E is especially effective against ozone, nitrogen dioxide and carbon monoxide. It helps the liver in its detoxification work and protects against poisons in food, water, air and drugs which interfere with tissue oxygenation. Vitamin A protects the mucous membranes; thus it is helpful in shielding against smog. Vitamin D is a specific in acute lead poisoning, just as calcium and magnesium help neutralize toxic substances in the body such as lead, mercury, strontium 90, cadmium and radioactive iodine.

We have found that people who suffer from migraine are high in copper and that their headaches decrease in incidence and severity when treated with a zinc supplement. In addition, the pill has been reported to cause migraine headaches, as it raises the copper level. Besides this, there is general agreement that the use of the pill may bring about elevated blood pressure and blood clots in the veins or arteries. As we know, copper is high in those who use tobacco. How, then, about the cigarette-smoking woman on the pill who drinks copper-loaded water and is also under stress (which depletes zinc)? Isn't she asking for an early heart attack or stroke?

With all this evidence there seems little doubt that it's supremely important to make sure we obtain, in one way or another, an adequate supply of the essential minerals and vitamins. It's nothing more or less than taking out a great big insurance policy on your health—both physical *and* mental.

5 🍁 What's Wrong with the Way We Eat?

Man is clearly what he eats, and the subject of nutrition has become almost as popular on the newsstands as sex. There's obviously growing awareness that despite the advances in medicine the American way of life has led us into "doing better and feeling worse." It is safe to say that half the people of the United States live on an inadequate diet, choosing the foods that are easiest to come by but often the least nutritious.

If technology hasn't been the answer, perhaps better health education is. Where does one go, however, after turning for the answers to one's doctor and finding him incapable of supplying them? The key, of course, to this vital information lies in the medical schools and undergraduate courses in human biology. Let us hope that the situation is improving.

Nutrition as a science was developed in the nineteenth century; at that time it was decided that "life is a chemical process." By the end of that century some aspects of nutrition had been discovered, but to this day we don't have all the answers where energy requirements are concerned. During the intervening years nutrition has developed many aspects—political, for one, and certainly

45

commercial. The food industries are well represented in every area, from the market basket to books. The great Madison Avenue sell is nowhere more apparent than in the way our young people are trained from babyhood by television to consume what Madison Avenue wants them to. (Currently there are efforts to control this through legislation, but they have so far been unsuccessful.) Since the average family knows little or nothing about nutrition, the profit motive wins out over the health factor most of the time.

There are enormous areas of nutritional controversy: coronary heart disease, cancer of the GI tract, osteoporosis, hypertension, cholesterol, fiber, vegetarianism, organic foods, breast feeding, refined sugar, salt and megavitamins. All pertinent questions will no doubt be resolved in time, given the technology and brains at work on the problems—but meanwhile the public is very understandably confused.

Ignorance is apt to breed doubts and superstitions and as a result we have some myths to dispel. For instance, there's a general belief that only meat gives us protein and that vegetables could never be the equal. This is quite erroneous. It's a matter of calorie density: a helping of broccoli has a very high protein value in proportion to the calories consumed. There's also the advantage that the calories are in a high fiber form. Another faulty idea is that it's desirable to have only one meal a day. This is decidedly not true; if you measure the utilization of calories, you find the most efficient way to fuel the body is by frequent meals, because the wider the spread of caloric intake, the more fat is turned into energy. Still another myth is that there is a dire necessity to augment the diet with cow's milk in order to acquire sufficient calcium. Again, not true; the requirements of calcium have been grossly overestimated. According to Dr. Keith Taylor of

Stanford Medical School 200 mg a day is adequate for bone development and dental requirements. The only reason for the huge consumption of milk is that people as dearly love it as they do junk food! In children it may *exclude* important nutrients.

Orthomolecular doctors have found many people to be allergic to one or more of the nutritious foods that modern society serves in almost constant repetition. These include milk, eggs, beef, wheat and corn products. This finding is hardly new; 2,000 years ago Lucretius wrote: "What is food to one is another's bitter poison." Susceptibility to allergies and additives, along with an empty calorie diet (one which supplies calories without nutrients), makes the individual more vulnerable to the stresses of everyday life. Obviously the removal of the offending food is necessary; it may even reduce the need for megadoses of nutrients. (Some allergies, however, are familial and sometimes independent of nutrition.)

Then take a good look at what's being *done* to our food: The food that starts in nutrient-deficient soil with chemical fertilizers spends harmful time in shipping and storage before it even gets to the processing plant. By the time all the chemicals are added, it has pretty well lost its vital nutrients. The processing retards food spoilage, so the canned and frozen meats and vegetables, prepared breads and cereals, refined flour and sugar, can remain attractive and succulent on supermarket shelves for considerable periods. This is what we call modern convenience.

Actually, this processing decreases the quality of foods drastically by removing the most important elements for nutrition. Vegetables, for instance, lose some of the water-soluble vitamins and heat-sensitive nutrients, some of the minerals, and some of the C and the A and folic acid. Freezing partially removes such trace elements as zinc, manganese and calcium from our green vegetables. (This explains why they retain their color when cooked.) The culprit in this case is the chelating agent EDTA, so widely used in food processing that we can't help but consume sizable amounts of it. Of course, the obvious solution is to grow your own produce, thus avoiding chemicals such as EDTA and pesticides. This is impractical for most of us. As for buying "organic" fruits and vegetables, it's impossible for the average person to know whether they were organically grown or not.

Good health food stores can serve as a source of untinkered foodstuffs, however. For instance, only there can you find unrefined vegetable oil; the vegetable oils in the markets which are light and clear are so because the nutrients which gave it its dark color have been removed. The vitamin E and lecithin, natural oxidants, were replaced with synthetic "preservatives." The same is true of whole wheat, of course. White flour has lost the wheat germ and everything else that contributes vital nutrients such as zinc, iron, chromium, manganese and the B and E vitamins. White flour keeps longer because of this; whole wheat must be used faster. Simple, isn't it? The same holds true with sugar, of course; the nutrients are all squeezed out in the various stages of processing, and what's left is gulped down in enormous quantities, to the detriment of health, figure and teeth.

When we don't get the necessary nutrients, the chromium, manganese, zinc and magnesium, the B_6 and E, we lack the ability to utilize all the calories in the refined flour and sugar. Chromium, for instance, plays a part in our ability to burn sugar; the loss of zinc can produce an excess of cadmium which in turn can, through a chain of events, cause high blood pressure.

So much for what's taken out of our food before we get it! Let's have a look now at what's put into it! The Food

and Drug Administration, that personification of bureau-
cracy, has been less than helpful in protecting our foods.
Aside from its longtime insistence that vitamin supplements are totally unnecessary, the FDA is so slow to
ascertain the safety of chemicals used in our processed
and synthetic foods that it's unwise to depend on it.
Many items on its GRAS (generally recognized as safe)
list have not been adequately tested over a sufficient period of time. So much for our consumer protection
agency!

Concerning the 2,500 to 3,000 food additives currently
in use and listed GRAS, how much do we know of their
cumulative effects? How much do we know about their
interaction with other additives and the resultant toxicity? How can we be sure the additive hasn't just been
taken off the GRAS list, unbeknown to us, as we're lay-
ing in a large supply of an item containing it?

The profit motive is most obvious in the best-known
of the additives, preservatives. Prolonging shelf life fat-
tens profits. Preservatives known as antimicrobial are
used to inhibit, or slow, the growth of bacteria and mold.
Antioxidants such as BHT and BHA (with their long, un-
pronounceable list of chemicals) we are told are necessary to keep fats and oils from becoming rancid. Actually,
unprocessed oils can be kept perfectly safely in the refrigerator. It's known that BHA and BHT are cumulative in
the body, but what's not known is the toxic effect of this.
Could these unnecessary preservatives be one of the
causes of cancer? We simply don't know. Paradoxically
enough, however, recent studies suggest they *might* have
a role in the suppression of cancer. Again, we simply
don't know.

We do have enough positive evidence to cause us to
fear the nitrites: they can be changed into cancer-causing
chemicals by the stomach acids or by heating. These po-

tentially dangerous preservatives are what you get when you succumb to that hot dog at the ball game or those luncheon meats, including ham, on the buffet table. And bacon should be just a memory; it's all been treated with nitrites and has certainly been heated! Both sodium nitrate and sodium nitrite are toxic at relatively low levels and can affect vulnerable consumers such as little children, the pregnant woman's fetus and persons suffering from anemia. These chemicals have had serious effects on some persons, and steps should be taken to ensure their safe use.

Then we have the antibiotics and hormones. These are fed to the unwitting public through their use with animals—either to promote growth or treat disease. They come to us in our milk and our meat, producing various undesirable effects such as a change in the intestinal flora and an increase of resistance to future necessary use of antibiotics to curb infections. Although the hormone DES has been banned, it is still used to enhance growth by means of animal implants of the hormone. Do we know if *this* is harmful? Not yet, not until studies are concluded. And in the meantime?

The stabilizer BVO (brominated vegetable oil) was banned in Sweden and England in the sixties, but we're still adding it to our soft drinks and snacks here in the United States. This even though BVO is known to be cumulative in tissue and that its long-term effects remain unknown. As with several other of these possibly lethal chemicals, there are safe alternatives that could be substituted.

Processing destroys the natural emulsifiers in foodstuffs; ergo, we have synthetic emulsifiers. It's the emulsifier that makes the water mix with the fats. Although synthetic emulsifiers haven't been tested with the other additives, it is thought they cause many complicated and serious events in the body—making it easier to absorb the cancer-producing additives, for example. So much for emulsifiers!

However, because they encourage the absorption of other agents, synthetic emulsifiers greatly increase our vulnerability to food colorings. The majority of these colorings are synthetic and thus must be "certified" by the FDA. These "certified" colors are almost all thought to be possible cancer-producing agents. Some, such as FD&C Orange Nos. 1 and 2, Red No. 1 and Yellow Nos. 1, 2, 3 and 4, were banned after their use was found to be definitely harmful. And Violet No. 1, which was stamped on meat to tell you about its safety, was found to be cancer suspect and subsequently banned in 1973.

At present there are eight certified food colorings allowed for use in anything the manufacturer chooses. These are Reds 2, 3 and 40, Blues 1 and 2, Green 3 and Yellows 5 and 6. Orange B, Red 4 and Citrus Red 2 have been restricted. For instance, it's okay to use Red 4 in maraschino cherries because who's going to eat that many? Children, for one. And Red 2 was banned in the Soviet Union after it was found to cause birth defects. It's in much of our ice creams, candies, baked goods, etc., that have a pink tinge, and in red soft drinks. Furthermore, although the International Union Against Cancer feels that Green No. 3 and Blue No. 1 are potential dangers, we're still using them widely. The coloring used in butter and margarine, Yellow No. 6, is considered safe although one study indicates an effect on the eye.

Artificial flavorings, as we know, are widely used. Most of them are completely synthetic; nevertheless, hardly any of these flavorings have been tested as to their effects on the human body. One of the most controversial, MSG (monosodium glutamate), is in canned soups, frozen dinners and, until recently, was even in baby food.

MSG excites the taste buds, thus its widespread commercial use. It also excites the nerve endings, possibly causing brain damage in babies and unpleasant symptoms in adults, especially after eating Chinese or Japanese food, both of which are heavily laced with it. It can cause dryness of the mouth and headaches and in arthritics it is likely to cause joint pain. However, because of its universal use in widely sold items, it is likely that big business will manage to keep it there. Sad, but true.

More than two-thirds of the products we find in our markets today weren't there prior to World War II. Not only have these new products tripled or quadrupled our food bill, but most of the older items have been tinkered with in some way. One must go to some effort now to secure good honest foodstuffs; unfortunately what's sold in the supermarket represents the easy way out to most people. Hot dogs, for instance, are somewhat of a staple in many homes. When you consider that they may be made up of the fatty parts of meat, usually rejected, and of fillers, water, spices, sodium nitrate, sodium ascorbate and glucona delta lactose and perhaps of some cereal or flour—do you really think this is what you want to feed your children? The mustard they pour on may be even more lethally dosed with chemicals, and the bun has been dosed to preserve its shelf life. As for ice cream, only the more expensive natural ice creams are free of a myriad of additives.

You would need a degree in chemistry to be able to understand the lists of ingredients on our products. Strong eyes, too: ingredients generally seem to be printed in infinitesimal type. They are always listed in order by quantity; you'll almost always find water or sugar at or near the top of the list and the nutrients far down. Packaged breakfast cereals are a good example: some cereals contain as much as 50 percent sugar. The food industry talks out of both sides of its mouth about giving consumers full, sensible and honest shopping information. It pays lip service to the notion of promoting health, but meanwhile it opposes every bit of legislation aimed at labeling or the reform of food-grading nomenclature. The food industry spends billions annually to promote junk foods; it designs supermarkets to trap shoppers into impulse spending.

Clearly, the adulterated foods now available to the consumer don't provide all the nutrients essential to optimal physical and mental health. Despite researchers' evidence that even the best diet today is inadequate, the FDA has slapped controls on the sale of nutrient supplements because they fear "health faddists" will receive overdoses. As Dr. Donald Davis, assistant professor of chemistry at the University of California at Irvine, says: "No normal daily amount of a vitamin supplement gives 10 percent of a lethal dose." Moreover, the individual concerned with the quality of his food is not usually a faddist, but merely someone who recognizes his needs.

Aside from additives, our faulty eating in general stems from overconsumption of saturated fat, dietary cholesterol, calories and sugar and salt. Of these, animal fat excess and salt excess are probably more dangerous to us than our enormous sugar excess. However, sugar is a risk we can avoid, along with the processed foods they're presented in which are high in saturated fat and salt. Diets high in animal fat and low in fiber seem to be connected to cancer of the colon, rectum and breast; these diets are also highly common to cardiovascular disease. We don't yet know exactly why this is true, but the cause and effect relationship is presently being studied.

6 🍁 How We Should Eat

We have all known for years that eating properly is essential to good health. First our mothers told us, then we were given little food charts at school, then Adelle Davis and others gave us reams more information. Why then, pray tell, is the American diet so perfectly awful? Why do at least 50 percent of the American people live on a junk diet that puts them on the verge of real malnutrition —poverty-level malnutrition, though the majority certainly aren't poor?

As pointed out in the previous chapter, for years we've been almost checkmated into our diet by the powerful food industry. The selection of foods is not instinctive in man; our eating habits are largely determined by our environments—which in our case includes radio, television and the rest of the mass media. The drastic changes in our eating habits since the turn of the century did not just happen. There must be reasons why the series of changes took place! In 1920 we were eating calories, fruits and vegetables. By 1950 we'd turned to animal protein and complex carbohydrates, and now our diet is made up of a heavy proportion of fats, salt and sugar. This is progress?

Two of the questions most frequently asked in doctors'

offices are "But what about my diet?" and "What should I be eating?" Rare indeed is an answer to these questions. For now, let's examine the basic ground rules of good nutrition for the average healthy person, one not suffering from a particular disease. We'll give suggestions of specific foods for specific diseases and disorders later on in this chapter.

Savarin wasn't far wrong when he wrote: "Tell me what you eat, and I will tell you what you are." How we eat determines to a large extent our successes and our failures; how we eat affects our personalities, our behavior, because our emotional and mental responses depend largely on our physical state. Sensible eating provides curative diets.

Our nutrient needs can be defined quite simply: we should be supplied with adequate protein, vitamins, minerals and trace elements, adequate fluid, carbohydrates and fats and fiber. But what *is* adequate? What proportion *is* necessary for optimum nutrition? Although we all know pretty much about the basic food groups, it's doubtful that many individuals know anything about particular needs—what foods are necessary for what functions. And what foods are necessary for *his* particular needs. From the standpoint of good nutrition and the good life, the individual's basic personality is important. Needs will vary according to personality traits; Susie Q., a stressed person, will need more vitamin C and trace elements, for instance, than Betty B., who makes her way through life in serenity. There can't be a rigid ruling about what and when we should eat; we need first to be enlightened and to adopt a reasonable attitude. After all, there's probably not a single statement that can't be contradicted by someone, somewhere!

Man gets his energy, is fueled by, carbohydrates, fats and protein. Therefore the body needs some of these foods daily: lean meat, fish or poultry; vegetables and fruits; whole grain cereals and breads; eggs if the cholesterol level permits. What a wide choice! If one can't choose a pleasing diverse diet from all these, he's certainly lacking in imagination. Why can't we try eating lower on the food chain, depending on the basic plant foods of the earth? Remember, all foods go back in a chain to the sun. Why can't we live more simply, slow down enough to really enjoy the taste of real food, make eating the social event it once was?

The traditional American diet is made up of proportionately high fat, high refined carbohydrates and low roughage or fiber. Even though the body's first need is for energy, most of us eat too *much* protein. For years there has been an emphasis on animal foods; the per capita increase in protein has been 83 percent in the last twenty years. Even poverty groups get more protein than they can use. Carbohydrate consumption, however, has dropped 50 percent since the beginning of the century. When you consider that the body's first need is for energy, you can understand malnutrition among those who don't get enough plant life; the lack of carbohydrates starves the body for energy. If carried to its most extreme, the body would start consuming its own muscle!

For this reason heavy emphasis should be placed on fruits and vegetables and grains. There should of course be protein, but not in the current quantities; the calorie intake will drop because of the added bulk. And whenever possible, let them be natural foods! It may be a little more trouble—they may be harder to find and take longer to prepare—but what a difference in nutrition! Sear the following list of vitamin- and mineral-rich vegetables, given in descending order of importance, in your memory.

Broccoli
Spinach
Brussels sprouts
Lima beans
Peas
Asparagus
Artichokes
Cauliflower
Sweet potatoes
Carrots

A compact, nutrition-packed diet is, it is hoped, the coming thing; food choices will be made intelligently, with due consideration given to the pleasure element.

There's so much evidence that we would benefit from reducing our meat intake that it must be emphasized. This doesn't mean cutting it out—it simply means that we would profit by getting along on less fat and smaller amounts of protein, while at the same time increasing the amount of vegetables and other high-roughage foods.

Fats and oils, both saturated and unsaturated, also occupy a too prominent place in our diets. The explanation of these two latter terms is somewhat complicated but worth understanding. All fatty substances are made up of atoms of carbon, hydrogen, and oxygen linked together in various ways. Saturated fat molecules have as many hydrogen and oxygen atoms as they can possibly hold. In a sense they're "saturated" with hydrogen; it is hydrogen saturation that makes most of them solid at room temperature. Fats "unsaturated" with hydrogen are usually liquid at room temperature—unless they've been partially hydrogenated to render them solid.

We all know the relationship between the saturated fats and cholesterol; the American Heart Association has clearly recommended a diet containing more unsaturated than saturated fats.

At a hearing of the Senate Select Committee on Nutrition and Human Needs, expert witnesses agreed that nutritional deficiencies and excesses—and in particular a high fat diet—appear to play a key causative role in cancer of the colon, stomach and breast. Dr. Ernst L. Wynder of the American Health Foundation said there is "a worldwide correlation" between colon cancer and fat consumption, with mortality rates high in countries such as the United States, Canada and Scotland and lower in Japan and Chile.

Another intriguing possibility comes from Dr. Gio B. Gori of the National Cancer Institute. Recent experiments have been made using nutrition as a direct form of cancer therapy. It is known, he has said, that tumors compete for nutrients in the body and that their nutritional needs differ from those of the "host." He further told the Senate Committee that "it appears that it may be possible to adjust available nutrients in the host so that the host may be fed and the tumor may be starved."

The best way to set your mind at rest concerning cholesterol is to have it tested, particularly if you're over fifty. The so-called normal range is from 140 to 280, but it is safest to keep it under 200. Many, many factors enter into cholesterol elevation, including mineral deficiencies —the lack of any number of things, such as magnesium, potassium, manganese, zinc, vanadium, chromium, selenium, vitamins C or E, niacin, folic acid or pyridoxine. Adequate magnesium is particularly essential in keeping cholesterol down, and zinc has also been found to be extremely valuable. Dr. Harold Petering and his associates at the University of Cincinnati Medical Center have found that blood fat levels decreased when blood zinc levels were increased. Vegetarians have been found to have lower cholesterol levels than those who eat meat, as plant foods and whole natural carbohydrates seem to have this effect. One wonders what the cholesterol levels were in the early part of the century!

Another widely discussed factor today is fiber, or the lack of it. Again we can blame the food industry for refining or milling out the bran and cellulose of plants, but it is ourselves we must blame if our lack of fiber is due to excessive meat intake and a deficiency of vegetables and fruits. The answer, of course, is less meat and more vegetables, with perhaps the addition of cereals such as unmilled bran or whole grains. A bowl of crunchy whole grain cereal with a few tablespoons of bran and wheat germ and topped with a large dollop of yoghurt makes a fine start to the day. I like popcorn as a fibrous breakfast; it's nutritious and makes a delicious breakfast cereal. You can pop it in advance and store it in cans.

Now, considering the major nutritional flaws we've discussed—additives, high fat, excessive meat consumption, lack of fiber—what is the answer as far as your diet is concerned? It would, it seems, boil down to a more heavily vegetarian diet, purer, more natural, simpler. Fresh foods, to start with; nothing frozen or canned or stored for weeks, but as fresh as one can manage. Less meat and more vegetables means lower cholesterol and higher fiber.

Vegetarianism, however, has its good news and its bad news. Common sense and some information are in order. The vegetarian concept has been around for a long time; through history people have turned away from meat for a variety of reasons. There are religious teachings; there are opponents of animal killing; and then there is the basic fact that meat is the most expensive food and as such is out of sight for the majority of the world's population. It is this latter fact that accounts for the high cholesterol of the affluent nations—the United States, Germany, France, for example. Some people have chosen a vegetarian regime out of concern for the environment, and some simply out of concern for their health. In *Diet for a Small Planet,* by Frances Moore Lappe, we find some interesting suggestions for eating with the health of the planet in mind as well as ours.

Our modern knowledge of biochemistry enables us to approach a more or less vegetarian diet with proper caution. A completely meatless diet, for instance, may lead to serious consequences. The protein and nutrient needs must be met! This caution may apply only to the true vegan, who eats no animal food or dairy products. The lacto-vegetarian drinks milk and eats cheese and butter, and the lacto-ovo-vegetarian also eats eggs as well as dairy products.

Obviously, the concern will be an adequate supply of protein, but actually this concern affects only the true vegan, and an intelligently planned vegetarian diet easily meets the protein requirement. However, another bad news possibility in the vegetarian diet is a possible deficiency of B_{12}, as this vitamin is found only in animal products. The consequences of this deficiency can be very serious anemia and degeneration of the spinal cord. Folic acid masks this deficiency, and because green vegetables contain folic acid, the B_{12} deficiency may go undetected until there's irreparable nerve damage. Also, most vegetarian regimes include very little vitamin D, which could be a problem in rainy or smoggy locales.

The most serious and probably least-known danger, however, is a deficiency of zinc. Meat is one of our main sources of zinc, and unless the diet contains lots of the other foods containing zinc, a deficiency is more than likely to occur. Sprouted grains, beans and seeds should be a part of everyone's diet in any case, as they help neutralize elements that antagonize zinc. Remember that one of the easily recognized signs of a zinc deficiency is the appearance of white spots on the fingernails. Another is stretch marks on the body. The vegetarian who thinks his other-world-like dreamy mysticism is contributed by his brown rice would do better to take a zinc tablet to feed the hidden zinc hunger that's making him light-headed.

The last bit of the bad news is that vegetarians may possibly get too much iron and even too many vitamins. Over a period of time an excess of iron can cause serious damage to the liver and heart, especially if the diet is poor in protein.

Allowing for these bad-news warnings, and emphasizing a need for B_{12} injections and zinc supplements, let's take a look at a diet that leans away from meat and toward vegetables, fruits and grains.

One of the major misunderstandings about protein is the belief that animal protein is superior to plant protein. Not so. Eggs, cheese, fish, milk and whole rice contain proteins that are of a better quality than those in meat; some plant foods, such as broccoli, contain a greater quantity.

The amino acids that are the building blocks of proteins come from both plant and animal foods, but the proteins of vegetables and cereals don't contain all the amino acids we need. This is why vegetarians must include some milk, cheese and eggs in their diet. Yeast, however, is the only plant food that contains all the amino acids, and this is a simple supplement that can be added to every meal. Brewer's yeast, in either tablet or powdered form, contains all the B vitamins needed to combat stress and for the utilization of carbohydrates, fats and proteins in the body. There is a delicious product made from brewer's yeast called Vegex, which, when stirred into a cup of hot water, becomes what you would swear is a rich beef broth.

These amino acids establish the quantity of the protein made available to our bodies—which, after all, is the crux of the matter. Oddly enough, it's the protein in that controversial egg that comes closest to filling the requirements of our body's amino acid pattern, and next best are milk, fish, cheese, whole rice, red meat and poultry. Certain foods, when eaten together, achieve a mutually complementing amino acid pattern. Certain plant foods, such as rice and beans, can be eaten together to give us splendid protein; *Diet for a Small Planet* has lots of suggestions pertinent here.

As to that controversial egg—well, there's a great deal to be said! The pros and cons go on and on, but we have some very definite ideas on the subject. We feel that the egg has been very much maligned and should be a part of our daily food—granted, of course, that our cholesterol level is normal. As mentioned before, a simple test is recommended for those of us over fifty and anyone else who might suspect high cholesterol owing to his diet.

To begin with, chicken eggs provide excellent food. The protein balance of the egg conforms better to the needs of your body than does any other food. Among its myriad virtues is its cost: it is the best value in proteins on the market. Add to this the fact that it provides us with choline, vitamin A, tryptophan, pyridoxine (B_6), biotin, folic acid, riboflavin, thiamin, pantothenic acid, selenium, zinc, phosphorus, calcium, sulfur and, last but not least, B_{12}, which, as we have pointed out, is necessary to the vegetarian because it is found only in animal products. The egg is high in protein, low in calories; it is one of the few foods that can't be tampered with before it reaches us, because it comes in its own container. The sulfur contained in the egg (which is what turns your silver spoon black) is essential to our bodies daily and not readily available in other foods. All in all, the egg has an almost perfect, complete balance of nutrients. We recommend two a day.

Granted, eggs are high in cholesterol, but before excluding them from the diet you'd be wise to take a very good look at the rest of your diet. The famous Dr. Roger Williams, former director of the Clayton Biochemical Institute at the University of Texas, holds that the cholesterol will be utilized if the rest of the diet contains the necessary trace elements. Cholesterol levels are lowered by adequate vitamin C, niacin, zinc, chromium, magnesium and other things such as good daily exercise and plenty of fresh vegetables or other natural carbohydrates. It's the junk food diet that encourages a high cholesterol reading; once one gets away from the saturated fats and hydrogenized products, eats smaller amounts of animal protein and gets lots of exercise, there's probably no reason in the world he can't eat eggs. (Real eggs, however —not the additive-packed Egg Beaters or their like.) If in doubt, by all means have your cholesterol tested. If it is normal, then by all means enjoy those eggs.

The heart patient, however, requires a special regimen regardless of cholesterol level. Be it heart attack, hypertension, stroke, whatever, his condition necessitates special nutrients. Not for him the fast food, quick, frozen, empty calorie diet; the heart needs minerals and vitamins to ensure efficient function. It needs constant amounts of magnesium, potassium, manganese, calcium, zinc, sulfur, selenium and phosphate. These minerals are best supplied by natural foods such as fresh fruits and vegetables, grains—and if permissible—eggs. Of these, potassium and magnesium are the most important and at the same time the hardest to come by. For instance, those great American standbys, the hot dog and soft drink, contain only empty calories and are almost devoid of potassium and magnesium—to say nothing of their saturated fats and carbohydrates. The cardiac patient needs this snack like a hole in the head!

The heart patient should use Morton's Salt Substitute, adhering as completely as possible to a salt-free diet. This substitute has a high potassium and phosphate content and contains no foreign preservatives. He should avoid Chinese and Japanese restaurants, because of their heavy hand with MSG, and dry roasted nuts. In addition to the regular vitamin supplements, an adequate further supply of A and E is essential for the heart patient. The latter vitamin, though controversial, is proving to be beneficial. Brewer's yeast will provide the selenium the heart needs, as well as many other elements.

As to diet, certain foods are particularly necessary for the heart patient. They are those rich in potassium: green leafy vegetables, wheat germ, citrus juice, beans, lentils, nuts, dates, prunes and fruits of all kinds. Magnesium is present in milk and eggshells. (Eggs, when not contra-indicated, can be soaked in vinegar for 24 hours to soften the shells, then thrown whole into a blender, thus retaining the magnesium and calcium of the shells along with the other values of the egg. The vinegar from the shell will have lost some of its sourness, and with milk added, the result is a highly nutritious eggnog.)

Leafy green vegetables and grains are our main sources of manganese. It's also in whole grain cereals, corn germ and bran and nuts, particularly walnuts. Cloves, carda-mom seeds and ginger also contain manganese, oddly enough. Atlantic oysters are the number one source of zinc, with herring a close second. Much less zinc is provided by hard clams, soft clams, fish roe, bran wheat germ, oatmeal, milk, nuts, peanut butter, whole rye and wheat.

Our best source of sulfur is the egg yolk, but strong-smelling foods such as garlic and onions contain appreciable amounts. Good food sources of selenium include garlic, liver, eggs and brewer's yeast. Vitamin C comes to us in a variety of ways such as broccoli, brussels sprouts, parsley, green peppers, and of course orange juice. Vitamin E is in the vegetable oils from seeds such as wheat germ and peanuts, green leafy vegetables, milk and eggs. Dairy products give us vitamin A, as do fish liver and animal liver, vegetables, apricots, peaches, bananas and cantaloupe.

There we have the foods for the heart patient to choose from! Its scope is so wide that such undesirables as saturated and animal fats will hardly be missed. In the back of this book you'll find some recipes created especially for the heart patient and utilizing these foods.

Another common disorder that responds to diet is the much talked of but little understood functional hypoglycemia. Its symptoms develop in response to food intake, so one could say that it is truly a dietary disorder! However, stress can induce it by making excessive demands on the adrenal gland. However, it is nutritionally inadequate foods that exert the subtle, complex and damaging stress on the organs of the body regulating glucose metabolism. Refined sugar is the worst offender; when the pancreas is repeatedly forced to handle large amounts of glucose from a diet rich in refined sugar, the pancreas becomes sensitized and hypoglycemia develops. The adrenal gland, striving to maintain the proper glucose level, becomes exhausted. Soon after a meal, blood sugar falls below the fasting level and the body craves sugar, thus producing the symptoms of functional hypoglycemia.

How many of us, only a few years ago, ever heard of hypoglycemia? The sharply rising incidence of it in modern times is no doubt due to the greatly increased consumption of sugar. But once this causative relation has been established, what do we do about it? Diet, as we've said, is of primary importance. A high protein diet is indicated, carbohydrate intake must be severely restricted and sugar has to be eliminated completely.

Vitamin and mineral supplements recommended are the B complex vitamins, A and C, manganese, choline, zinc and chromium. Exercise is also an important part of the treatment of hypoglycemia. Patients on increasingly vigorous daily exercise find their symptoms improved.

Then we have the hypoglycemic diet, originally designed by Dr. Seale Harris, who first discovered that the pancreas can overproduce insulin. The following lists give a very clear idea of what to eat and what to avoid.

FOODS ALLOWED

All meats, poultry, fish and shellfish (with the exception of processed products such as lunch meat which contains a carbohydrate extender)
Dairy products: eggs, milk, butter, cheese
Margarine
Oils, preferably safflower, cold pressed
Whole grain bread or protein bread
Nuts such as walnuts, almonds, peanuts
Peanut butter without sugar
Soybeans and soybean products
Decaffeinated coffee, weak tea, herb teas, mineral water

FOODS TO AVOID

Sugar in any form—white, brown, whatever
Pastas: macaroni, noodles, spaghetti, etc.
Polished rice
White bread, buns, muffins
Pie, cake, other pastries
Ice cream, candy, dates
Cola and other soft drinks
Alcohol in all forms
Coffee and strong tea
Packaged junk foods (read the labels)

FOODS TO BE USED SPARINGLY

These include complex carbohydrates such as oatmeal, Wheatena, Shredded Wheat, brown rice, barley, potato, lentils, millet, dried fruits. Honey and molasses intake should be limited, and saccharine can be used as a substitute for sugar but only if very limited in quantity and frequency.

Actually training oneself to do without sugar is infinitely simpler than it sounds. After a while the taste buds respond to fruits, nuts and cheeses just as pleasurably as they did to chocolate ice cream. An apple with a bit of good Brie can make a wonderful end to a meal.

As mentioned earlier, my clinical reputation has been based mainly on my work in schizophrenia. And here again we find the answers to human diseases and disorders lying in nutrients! Our discovery of the almost miraculous efficacy of zinc and B_6 in dealing with schizophrenics is one of science's great breakthroughs in mental health. All through the six differentiations of schizophrenia, we've found these nutrient deficiencies, and the simplicity of treatment for this crippling mental disease is almost staggering. Also, we see how serious can be the results of zinc and B_6 deficiency! (And how easily avoided.)

For this reason certain foods high in these nutrients are certainly in order for those with emotional problems and disturbances and mental disorders. Foods high in these nutrients include brewer's yeast, bananas, lima beans, beef liver, roasted peanuts, sweet potatoes for the pyridoxine; seafoods, nuts and seeds such as sunflower or pumpkin, and leafy green vegetables for the zinc.

As to the actual purchase and preparation of the foods you eat, remember that the freshest, most natural, unpolluted foods are what you're after. When you go shopping, concentrate on your knowledge of what constitutes a balanced diet; selecting things at random just because they're there and look nice is playing Madison Avenue's game. It's not a bad idea to shop after a meal, when your appetite isn't so apt to lead you astray, and by all means take your glasses with you so you can read that tiny print on labels listing ingredients. As a matter of fact, try to avoid using canned products—although this is of course not always possible. It is possible, however, to speed past the shelves of Danish pastries and other breakfast temptations on your way to the fresh fruits and vegetables.

One last word of warning, first: although the benefits and delights of plant foods are practically infinite, certain dangers must be pointed out. Most fruits and vegetables need little or no cooking, and are, in fact, more nutritious when eaten raw. However, there are a few that require special care in preparation. The legume family (lima beans, lentils, soybeans and others) contain a variety of dangerous toxins that become harmless when sprouted or cooked; raw lima beans and other legumes have been reported to be fatal. Green peas and chick peas contain, in very small amounts, a toxin resistant to heat, but many people consume both these vegetables with no ill effects whatsoever. Uncooked fava beans are to be avoided; raw rhubarb leaves have excessive oxalic acid and can cause kidney damage. Raw cabbage, kale, watercress can be a contributing factor in goiter, and raw nutmeg is a psychedelic drug which, in overdose, can also be fatal.

On the other hand, certain commonly available foods are very high in antitoxic properties. Soured milks such as yoghurt and acidophilus neutralize poisons such as DDT and strontium 90, thus minimizing their damaging effects. Kelp is also some protection against radioactive fallout substances such as strontium 90 and radioactive iodine (present mostly in milk), to which most of us are subjected today. In addition, lecithin neutralizes poisons such as DDT, drugs, nitrites and mercury. Brewer's yeast is the best natural protective food with which to fight pollution; it helps your liver in its detoxification work and provides a definite protection against lethal radiation doses. All the above will protect you not only against environmental poisons but also from disease by increasing your resistance.

Back at the produce counter: make sure your market brings the fruits and vegetables in daily! They lose their vitamins and minerals very, very quickly! Choose with your body's special needs in mind, and refrigerate produce as soon as you get home, to preserve the nutrients. The crisper of your refrigerator was put there for this purpose; use it.

Choose your protein, remembering you don't need as much as you've been conditioned to think. It may be a breast of chicken or a piece of fish; it may be a lovely handful of mushrooms. Whatever, just make sure it's as fresh as it can be, and make haste to refrigerate it.

Your cooking utensils are an important part of the picture also. Surely by now you realize you mustn't use any copper; there's also evidence that aluminum should be avoided (including, alas, the foil). Pots of baked enamel on heavy iron, commonly used by the French and Belgians, are good for both purity and heat conduction. And even your knives are important. It seems vitamin C is easily oxidized by metal contamination during the processing of foods; a steel knife quickly becomes dull if used for slicing lemons. (The iron ends up in the lemon juice!) Stainless steel is better, and a plastic knife is best.

Steam vegetables in a colander or French steamer. Of course you'll save the small bit of water used in steaming to add to future soups or stews.

Use salt substitute and herbs for seasoning; you can make a very good salad dressing with oil, vinegar, dill weed and Vegesalt, a tasty commercial product. And this is where you can use that eggshell soaked in vinegar and pulverized in the blender; you'll have added magnesium and calcium and other trace elements to your salad. The vinegar from the eggshell will of course contain some trace elements, thus adding even more nutrition to your salad dressing or homemade mayonnaise.

Keep the liquid you've saved from steamed vegetables tightly bottled and refrigerated; it will retain its valuable potassium and other minerals for several days. Besides being added to soups or stews, it may be used as a cold drink or even as the liquid in which to cook cereals. Don't ever throw *anything* away that contains trace minerals and vitamins! With a little ingenuity everything can be utilized in one way or another.

Raw vegetable juice is a marvelous source of important trace minerals. A combination of carrot, parsley, celery and spinach juice will supply a great wallop of potassium. Raw potato juice has a high content of potassium, sulfur, phosphorus and chlorine. Lettuce juice has great quantities of iron and magnesium. In fact, raw vegetable juices provide our best natural source of most minerals. They can be mixed with broth or Vegex to make a soup.

While we're on the subject of liquids it might be wise to consider our drinking water. In the first place, it is vital to drink *enough* water—literally vital, that is. In the second place, it's important that it be good water—and in our age of polluted, contaminated water supplies, that's not all that easy. If you must use bottled water, don't use distilled; it will deprive you of all the valuable mineral and organic properties of drinking water. Bottled mineral water is very good; it has mineral content as well as taste and may have curative powers. The price is a disadvantage, however.

Soft water is well known to be undesirable as drinking water. Extensive studies both here and abroad have shown that where people drink hard water (which means a higher mineral content), there is a lower incidence of heart disease, tooth decay and diabetes. Soft water also increases the amount of copper leaking in from copper pipes.

To summarize, let's say we should eat more simply, lower on the food chain, more naturally. We should avoid all processed, tinkered food products; we should learn to cook in the most efficient way to preserve the maximum benefits of our foods. We should accept the fact that we don't need as much protein as we thought; we should cut way down on meat and introduce substitutes for it. We should increase our vegetable and fruit intake, thereby providing ourselves protein as well as the needed fiber. And let's get back to *enjoying* our food! Let's make each meal a highlight of the day.

7 🍁 There's No Trick to Weight Control

There are enormous areas of controversy in medicine today: coronary heart disease, hypertension, cancer of the GI tract, osteoporosis, cholesterol, salt, refined sugar, fiber, vegetarianism, organic foods, breast feeding and megavitamins. The most controversy, however, rages over how to control body weight. As George Mann said: "The holy grail of medicine is a safe and comfortable way to lose excessive body fat." Heaven knows that everyone has had a crack at it; fortunes have been made on everything from pills to elaborately presented routines. Sometimes it seems as if a new fad diet is born every week, with hordes of the overweight rushing to try what they're sure will be *the* one. The constant march of new weight-reducing schemes testifies both to the ingenuity of the human mind and to the average dieter's lack of perseverance. Not to mention the old achievement-without-effort syndrome.

Just how helpful or harmful are these diets? Well, consider the Atkins and Stillman diets. Their low carbohydrate content tends to intoxicate; it brings on nausea, an oddness in the head and a resultant loss of appetite. To eliminate carbohydrates from the diet is to induce an

72

abnormal metabolism, which could lead to permanent cellular damage. When the body balance is restored—before, it is hoped, a rise in the uric acid causes damage—the body weight returns to its former level. Another disappointment! The Simeons diet, however, is a real rip-off. Injections of the urine of pregnant women—quite expensive, perhaps because of our nearly zero population growth—are given. The regimen allows only 500 calories a day, which would reduce anyone. The Zen macrobiotic diet is in the main an expression of people striving for something, and there have been some bad results from this one—including death. In the case of the Cider Vinegar, Lecithin, Kelp and B$_6$ Diet, only the last named could affect weight loss, because it aids in fluid loss. The list is endless; there's the Ice Cream Diet, the Drinking Man's Diet, the Sweet Tooth Diet, the Mayo Diet (no connection with the famous clinic). These diets will, because of limited caloric intake, cause weight loss, but the price is much too high. Our bodies simply must have the nutrients supplied by carbohydrates, fats and proteins in proper balance; any number of disasters can result from the lack of these vital nutrients. On the other hand, some products have a preponderance of ingredients we could better live without. A product called Naturade, for instance, lists as the first ingredient in its otherwise long list of essential nutrients, sodium. Who needs sodium as the main ingredient of something that's to be his only food intake? After that is calcium and fibers, then pre-digested protein, and eventually one finds all the essential vitamins and minerals. (I'm sure everyone knows by now that ingredients are listed in order of quantity in the product.)

As we have said, ignorance is apt to breed doubts and superstitions. Some people labor under the misapprehension that calories don't count. This is completely in error; there is no way a healthy person won't gain weight when fed more calories than he burns up. All quick-cure diets fail to treat nutritional practices as part of one's total pattern of living. This applies to all the fad diets, with the exception of Weight Watchers. Weight Watchers is based on sound nutritional principles and is expected to become a life-style.

Vegetarianism isn't really a fad; it can be an acceptable diet. Do you ever see any fat vegetarians? It is perfectly possible to acquire an adequate amount of protein from a vegetarian diet; for instance, green vegetables, particularly broccoli, have a high protein content relative to the calories. The whole grains add protein, and in fact we could very possibly subsist on wheat protein if our animal proteins were no longer available.

Diets notwithstanding, the fact remains that a huge number of us fight a lifelong battle against overweight. We're all well aware of the threat to our health in added poundage and most of us care quite a lot about how we look. The problem is essentially so simple, of course. We supply the body with more calories than it can burn up and we get fat. We cut back the caloric intake and we get thin. Caloric needs vary, of course, according to body build, age (the young need more calories because they're growing), energy usage, and so on.

As we've pointed out, the dieter must make sure he is adequately supplied with all the essential nutrients. This means carefully selected foods that, while supplying minerals and vitamins, will add a minimum of calories. Empty calories are the dieter's worst enemy, and if he can establish a lifelong pattern of avoiding them, he's won half the battle. How easy it is to nibble on a few potato chips as long as they're sitting there; how tempting to butter a few pieces of that French bread while you wait for dinner to arrive; how right it would seem to have another glass of wine. Those shelves and shelves of tasty snacks and crackers, empty of food value and doctored with preservatives, are something you must simply become blind to. Remember, every mouthful must contribute nutritional value to your diet. All excess calories will be converted to body fat. Bear in mind that refined sugar is the emptiest carbohydrate of all. Find some other pleasure to replace the eating of junk foods—even if that pleasure is slightly unacceptable socially. (You can always give it up when you're slim and svelte again.)

Two pounds a week is the most sensible, realistic goal for the dieter. This goal can be reached by most people on a regimen of 1,000 calories a day, roughly 300 calories a meal plus a snack or two. One thousand calories should be enough to keep body and soul together; yet it is stringent enough to take off two pounds a week.

The trick, however, is to make those calories count. An egg and a piece of bread are equal in calories; each has 75. Is a slice of bread nutritious enough to grow a baby chick in 21 days? Choose well from the basic food groups described in Chapter 6, leaning on the proteins, vegetables and fruits, the whole grain breads and cereals. Cut down on the fats you use in cooking; avoid *all* refined carbohydrate foods. Try a little honey or molasses to sweeten things instead of sugar or saccharine. The former two contain an appreciable amount of trace elements.

The best meal plan for weight loss is an adequate breakfast, light lunch or nutritional low-calorie snack, and a modest dinner that is high in protein and low in fat. Some special cases, such as hypoglycemics, fare better on six small meals a day, and as this might pose a problem for most of the working public, these meals can be portable. A briefcase, a flight bag, a brown paper bag, can carry such valuable appetite quenchers as hard-boiled eggs, cottage cheese, raw vegetables, fruits, nuts and seeds. Perhaps when you know a snack is at hand you'll be less likely to dream of French-fried potatoes and apple pie à la mode. You might even carry a thermos of hot bouillon.

Cabbage and lettuce, cut in a wedge, can be eaten out of the hand as a picnic-style snack. Lunch needn't be a sandwich with too much bread and mayonnaise; lunch might be a chicken breast or drumstick, a hard-boiled egg, a piece of low-fat cheese, a piece of fruit and nuts. (Count 5 calories for each nut you eat.) Perhaps most important of all, approach the kitchen, or maybe in the first place the market, with a wary, skimpy eye. Nine times out of ten too much food is purchased, cooked and *eaten.* The idea of cooking just enough to allow all a small portion with no chance of coming back is almost un-American! However, with prices the way they are, and apparently are going to be, it seems as if we'll necessarily come to preparing adequate servings, no more, no less. The only things you want to see when you open the refrigerator door for a snack is a crisper full of carrot, celery and green pepper sticks!

What about thirst, you ask? All the soft drinks are full of sugar and additives; alcohol is a no-no carbohydrate. Remember that wonderful drink from your childhood, a tall glass of cold water? It's available to us as in almost no other country in the world, and it's cheap without calories. Besides, water has the benefit of decreasing hunger pangs because it washes the acids from the stomach, at the same time washing out excess salt, which gives us fluid retention. On the matter of empty calories, are you aware that the kinds of soft drinks consumed in this country from 1960 to 1975 increased from 1,897 to 9,476?

For most of us dinner is the main meal of the day, the one where we're together with family or friends for sharing a meal. If your will is particularly weak, perhaps you'd better for a while forgo the companionship of those who either don't need to diet or don't want to. Seek out someone who's trying, like you, to live on 1,000 calories a day and make a project out of it. You might even have a few side bets going on who's going to reach the desired goal fastest. In any event, *plan* your dinner *yourself:* don't rely on the hit-or-miss method of thinking you can pick and choose from what others have supplied.

It's always a good idea to start with a green salad, as it provides fiber to fill your stomach somewhat and also to alleviate constipation—to say nothing of the nutrients provided. Then it's not a bad idea to have a cup of bouillon, because it cuts down some on the appetite. (The French always have many small courses, and in spite of their reputation for gourmet fare, one doesn't see as much obesity there as here.) Then your small piece of fish, poultry or meat, in order of desirability. It's been broiled, of course, and is accompanied by a small serving of steamed broccoli and another of steamed carrots—just as an example. Perhaps you might have a little lemon juice and safflower oil on the vegetables, as you did on the salad. Perhaps you'll find a sprinkling of herbs and a little Vegesalt or salt substitute more to your liking. For dessert your carbohydrate appears in the form of a fruit, perhaps joined by a small piece of low-fat cheese. Now really, is there anything wrong with that dinner?

There's no reason you can't be exactly as you want to be, and if that means thin, *get* thin. The motivation to establish a goal comes from within you, nowhere else. The doctor may tell you to lose ten pounds, but absolutely nothing's going to happen until you make up your mind that thin is what you want to be. There are many groups and establishments that can set up a regime for you, but none greatly improve on that which you decide on and set up for yourself. You can even, if you can afford it, go to one of the fat farms where the disciplining will be done for you—but what about after you come home? No, the answer to setting up a lifetime pattern of eating for fitness and vigor lies deep within yourself. There may be cases of extreme obesity coupled with emotional problems which necessitate psychiatric help, but by and large it's up to *us* to do it ourselves!

Exercise is a double-edged tool in weight loss. Not only is it essential for the burning of calories and the healthful toning of the body, but it serves to keep one occupied and away from those snacks. In fact, the busier one is, the faster the time passes, the easier the diet regime becomes. So set yourself a regular routine of exercise. Perhaps one might begin by getting up a half hour earlier every morning and going through a rigorous set of exercises. A phonograph record with a good stimulating beat provides the pace, and the length of the record provides the time span. These exercises should include a five-minute warm-up of kicking and arm swinging, much like the current disco dancing. Bouncing vigorously back and forth from one leg to the other promotes the circulation up those legs to the heart; so do also jumping jacks. The rhythm of the recording keeps your pace up and before you know it you're very warm and breathing hard. Then go on to more exercises on the floor, such as getting on hands and knees and kicking the leg out rapidly to the side, as high as you can raise it. Then the other leg. Sitting up with legs spread, alternate touching toes on the opposite foot at a rapid pace, and then lie back on your elbows and kick out vigorously, heels extended. Follow this with about 20 pushups and 30 sit-ups and you should feel glowing and fit—and ready for a shower.

Take up other exercise for fun, such as bicycling, tennis or the omnipresent jogging. Plan to spend the time before dinner, formerly occupied with a cocktail or wine,

outside having a good time with a friend. A friend, that
is, who's aiming in the same direction as you are. Incidentally, though you probably have never thought of it,
sex is good exercise too. Perhaps the friend might stay for
a diet dinner and then work off 400 calories with you! In
other words, reach for your mate instead of your plate!

So—after you've chosen wisely from the basic food
groups, with particular attention to a balanced combination of protein and carbohydrates, and when you've established your likes and dislikes so that you're
comfortable with the regimen—then the trick is to stay
just *under* the sufficient amount. This is probably your
1,000 calories a day, which will drop your two-pounds-a-
week.

However, even this slight limitation means you must
watch those essential nutrients; it's more important than
ever during weight reduction. On the other hand, some
nutrients can even help in your effort. Take a daily
multipurpose vitamin pill (no copper), five brewer's yeast
tablets three times a day (remembering to start with two
and add gradually), 20 mg of zinc gluconate twice a day
and B_6 twice a day. The multipurpose guards against any
deficiencies, the brewer's yeast gives you your B complex
vitamins and the sugar-burning "glucose tolerance factor." As we're all probably zinc deficient, the zinc supplement may alleviate one of your hidden hungers, and B_6
should be taken with the zinc because they work together; in addition, B_6 works on its own toward weight
reduction. Depending on individual needs, the amount of
B_6 could range from 50 mg A.M. to 200 mg A.M. without
harmful effect.

Why is overweight such a factor in our American way
of life? Why is the average American from 15 to 20
pounds over the weight most beneficial to his health?
The reasons are myriad, ranging from our affluence to

the powerful lobbies of the food industry. In 1900 we ate more, to be sure—but we weighed less because we exercised more. We can blame the automobile for much of that one! However, it is hoped that education will lead to better national eating habits. Who knows—perhaps one day soon we'll have a Health and Obesity lobby!

8 🍁 Knitting the Raveled Sleave of Care

Sleeplessness has to be a modern complaint. I just can't picture the peoples of bygone times wandering around their caves, huts or castles in the middle of the night, seeking restful oblivion. The great majority of us over "a certain age" suffer from insomnia at least a part of the time, and the rest are likely to complain of unrestful sleep, too early awakening and other problems *ad infinitum*.

It's impossible to describe the exact nature of sleep; scientists have discovered activities that occur during sleep such as REM (rapid *e*ye *m*ovement) and have measured the brain's electrical activity during sleep, but as to the precise reason we fall asleep and stay asleep—the answers are difficult.

However, new research into insomnia has brought some interesting facts to light. Individual needs vary much more widely than heretofore thought; the average adult sleeps seven to nine hours a night, but then there are the few who need only four, while some must have twelve. And nature, discounting problems, will take the sleep she needs. Don't worry about getting too little, and don't turn the four-hour sleeper into an eight-hour sleeper with pills!

Those who feel they have sleep difficulties should go to bed only when really tired; if the day's work doesn't leave you tired enough, go for a walk before bedtime, a brisk walk, to invite fatigue. Walking is a simple and convenient activity and can help smooth over problems. Above all, don't go to bed when you're tense and anxious; don't go to bed burdened with worries. Sit up and do your worrying in a chair, then try to read something to put your mind in a more peaceful condition. A nightcap, widely thought to be the answer, isn't likely to promote a good night's sleep, because alcohol releases adrenaline into the blood, which is likely to wake you up about four hours later.

There's bad news and good news, however, for the many who feel they simply must resort to artificial means to get a good night's sleep. The sleeping pill prescription is undoubtedly the most frequently filled prescription today; some five million are filled each year for the most popular capsule. When you think of the numbers of other prescribable and over-the-counter items you realize how desperate a great number of people are about getting enough sleep. It's safe to say that almost all sleeping preparations are harmful in the long-term usage; perhaps the only relatively harmless ones are the two generic aspirin, which have been found to be just as effective in promoting sleep as the leading tranquilizers. Many of the sedatives sold over the counter, as two doctors recently warned a House health subcommittee, contain a common drug linked with cancer in animals. In addition, some of these nonprescription aids contain a substance that reacts with the nitrites in the stomach to form one of the most potent cancer-causing agents known to man.

And now for the good news! In view of these facts, isn't it great to know that we've found a trio of vitamins that produce healthy, sound, undrugged sleep? These wonderful sleep vitamins are vitamin C; inositol, which is one of the B complex; and vitamin B_6. Aside from those for whom insomnia is an imagined disorder or a symptom of another disorder, vitamin therapy can provide the safe, comfortable answer.

C's usefulness comes from its ability to combat our old friend who wears many guises, anxiety. Our group has found through studies that vitamin C acts as an antianxiety agent; they now use it in the general nutritional program to treat excessively nervous patients. The effect of vitamin C lasts for six hours, which of course is helpful when it is used as a relaxant.

The second sleep vitamin is the little-known inositol. It comes from corn through a separating process; little is known about man's needs for or deficiencies of inositol, but we do know that because of its presence in the body, particularly the brain, it must have an important significance. What we do know, however, from studies at the Brain Bio Center is that inositol has an antianxiety effect similar to that of Librium or meprobamate. Inositol is sedative; it solves many anxiety and insomnia problems. This little wonder vitamin is available at health food stores in tablets containing 250 mg, 500 mg and 625 mg. It might be necessary to experiment to see which size you need, but for sleep perhaps you'll need the maximum dose while for daytime jitters the minimum. Foods that contain appreciable amounts of inositol include wheat germ, barley, beef, green peas, cabbage and grapefruit, beef heart and beef liver.

The third vitamin for sleep is B_6. This, pyridoxine, is one of the most important vitamins. It's so necessary to the body's workings that a deficiency can produce all kinds of mental and physical problems. The need for B_6 supplement in a healthy, unstressed individual is determined in part by his protein consumption, but by and large the need in adults is about 50 mgm, with much more need under stress. We all know that dreaming, and particularly dream recall, is an important part of our sleep pattern. Studies at the Brain Bio Center indicate that dream recall can serve as a yardstick for measuring B_6 deficiency. Fifty mg could be a starting point to produce dreams; if no recall occurs, the dosage can be doubled.

I myself have found that I seem to need 50 mg of B_6 each morning to produce normal dreaming at night. Because I lead a stressful life at the Brain Bio Center, directing its operations and seeing patients, in addition to my writing, this helps my normal sleep. However, when on vacation I find I must halve the dose or I dream too much —which can of course cause restlessness or even wakefulness. Others, on the other hand, need upward of 100 mg a day to achieve the same dreaming; it's another very individual need.

In addition to recommending these three sleep vitamins, we can add a few somewhat obvious suggestions. A hot bath, as we know, has a soporific effect. It relaxes the muscles and produces a mental state of drowsiness. This, coupled with a cup of hot milk, can produce a good night's sleep. Not only does milk neutralize stomach acid, but it contains tryptophan, an amino acid that some scientists think is sleep-inducing.

So, armed with the old-fashioned and the new-fashioned remedies (and of course having eliminated coffee and tea) and with the knowledge that you probably don't need as much sleep as you think you do, relax and allow all these factors to fight the problem for you. Sweet dreams!

9 🍁 The Alcoholic

In 1956 the American Medical Association at long last designated alcoholism as a bona fide, treatable disease. Before that it was a condition that was either ignored altogether or swept under the carpet; families having an alcoholic among them suffered in silence and endured the tragic consequences because there was literally nowhere to go for help.

Now that it has been recognized as the fourth most serious threat to American health, we're coming to grips with it in the medical field; and all signs point to a day when this challenging problem can be brought under control. Most of us are aware of the statistics, if vaguely —that the national cost of alcoholism is $15 billion a year, that the suicide rate is 58 percent higher in alcoholics, that 28,000 alcohol-related automobile accidents occur each year and that the alcoholic's life span is cut short by 11 years.

Of the 9 million alcoholics who need treatment, there are those few who almost make it funny; as we know, many alcoholics are brilliant writers and wits. W. C. Fields, for instance, said, "Always carry a flagon of whiskey in case of snakebite and furthermore always carry a small snake." And "A woman drove me to drink, and I never even wrote to thank her." F. Scott Fitzgerald wrote some of his most poignant books while in the throes of alcoholism, along with many others of our best writers. Unfortunately, their lives, and therefore their output, were always cut short.

The damage to the human body by alcohol is inestimable. We all think first of cirrhosis of the liver, which of course is usually an irreversible killer. When the liver can no longer perform its assigned job of detoxifying the poisons in our bodies, we've had it. However, there are endless more subtle effects such as impairment of judgment, control and learning ability and the resultant behavior problems. This last is of course what we see most of, and what causes the heartbreak in families. Alcohol damages the kidneys and depletes the blood sugar, producing hypoglycemia.

Needless to say, the alcoholic loses his capacity to function efficiently and inevitably suffers first the loss of the respect of his peers, then his self-respect, followed usually by his job, then perhaps by his family. Unfortunately, the alcoholic is almost impossible to help while on this downward trend; his wife or family is usually powerless to reach him. In most cases the help must be sought by the alcoholic himself before the trend can be reversed, and in more cases than not this realization of need for help comes too late.

So far the most effective help for the alcoholic has come from Alcoholics Anonymous (AA). With his nutritional deficiencies and neurological syndromes he simply hasn't the strength to cope with his problem on his own, and AA offers the person-to-person guidance that can boost his morale, make him feel he's not alone in the world with his problem. Of course he has to raise his hand and ask to be helped, which is sometimes very difficult, sometimes impossible. But the daily or nightly meetings that are available in almost all our cities offer the participating help and friendship the alcoholic needs to go on to a more effective cure.

In our society the disease is more often than not politely ignored; wives cover up as best and as long as they can. Excuses for bizarre behavior are made; accidents are hushed up. The family doctor should, however, be able to spot the symptoms, which range from gastrointestinal complaints to heart palpitations. The conditions common to almost all alcoholics are nutritional deficiencies, dehydration and hypoglycemia. Sometimes, however, the alcoholic is gifted with an unusually strong constitution and manages to escape these latter symptoms. We all know people who manage to drink themselves into insensibility night after night and still leap bright-eyed out of bed in the morning. So far—but in the meantime the damage to brain cells and life-style creeps on, and by the time help arrives it's often too late.

How is the alcoholic best treated? Assuming, that is, that he has admitted his problem and joined AA. If he opts for psychiatric treatment it will be through talk therapy; medicine, on the other hand, will seek to deal with the illness first and later seek answers for the psychological problems. This latter approach has proved to be more successful than psychotherapy alone, as the alcoholic must have stopped drinking before that sort of treatment can be effective. "Never mind my parents' divorce when I was six," he pleads. "I need help now."

How is the problem best approached by medicine? Enormous time and effort have been spent attempting to find a cure for alcoholism. The research has ranged from nutrient therapy to psychedelics such as LSD, with varying results. A drug called Flagyl, discovered in 1964, lessens the desire for alcohol, but any alcohol imbibed on top of it will make the user extremely ill. He'll have abdominal cramps, nausea and vomiting, which would probably be all right if there weren't also possible health hazards. In addition, the effect is temporary; the drug doesn't have lasting effect.

Antabuse is somewhat like Flagyl, in that after dosage with it the smallest amount of alcohol will make the person extremely ill. Antabuse has proved helpful to the alcoholic who has made up his mind to stop drinking and needs this added deterrent; the effects are so extreme, however, that it's inadvisable for use by a person who lives alone, because any relapse from alcohol abstention could be extremely dangerous.

The use of barbiturates and tranquilizers can pose the danger that one addiction may replace the other. Although under extremely controlled conditions dry drugs can be helpful in the treatment of alcoholism, the fact remains that there is always the danger of addiction. The use of drugs has become so common as to be almost acceptable socially; yet we know full well the disastrous results of drug abuse and addiction.

Sleep-producing drugs, no matter what kind, depress enzyme systems in the brain so that fuel accumulates. The continued use of artificial "downers" as a substitute for alcohol will only produce an opposite "upper reaction" when the accumulated fuel burns too rapidly in the brain. These depressants are habit forming, so that the patient can't stop taking them without becoming seriously ill; they can lead to the D.T.'s, convulsions, bizarre behavior and abnormal thinking. Barbiturates are also extremely dangerous to the suicide-minded alcoholic; often they are the cause of death through accidental overdose. We all know that their effects are additive with alcohol and that the combination has killed a well-publicized many.

If you drown your sorrows in strong alcoholic drinks, you will get the reaction you expect. If your brain, however, is susceptible to total electrical discharge (epilepsy), you may have what's called a "rum fit" four to six hours after falling asleep dead drunk. Some susceptible people may have major seizures only under these circumstances, so they soon learn to avoid strong alcoholic drinks (otherwise, for one thing, their driver's licenses would soon be lost to the epilepsy label). Dr. Harris Isbell of Lexington, Kentucky, a great pioneer in the study of narcotics, has produced these fits in volunteers by careful round-the-clock overdosing with various downer drugs —alcohol, chloral, barbiturates and some of the newer downers such as Doriden, Noludar, Dalmane, Placidyl, Quaalude, Triclos and Lotusate. Addiction is the ever-present danger with all these commonly used drugs; even the antianxiety drugs such as Valium, Librium, Tranxene, Serax and meprobamate are addicting when the dose is increased.

Many misconceptions about alcoholism are gradually disappearing. We're finally beginning to realize that genetic and biochemical deficiencies may cause some alcoholic abuse and to treat the disease from this viewpoint. As far as treatment goes, the patient must resolve from the beginning to face the problem completely. He can be dried out over and over, each time thinking he's cured—only to start the whole cycle again.

The alcoholic should select a doctor or clinic capable of and willing to give him a biochemical diagnosis. The doctor, if he realizes that the patient didn't just sit down and decide to become an alcoholic, will look for the biochemical quirk that tipped the balance. The tests he should be given include: blood histamine levels; serum copper and zinc level to determine copper excess or zinc deficiency; blood spermine level or five-hour glucose tolerance test to detect hypoglycemia; allergy questionnaire, including yeast, hops, sugars, which may disclose cerebral allergy; psychometric tests such as the Experiential World Inventory, Hoffer-Osmond Diagnostic Test, Minnesota Multiphasic Personality Inventory to indicate disperceptions, paranoia, hypochondriasis and sociopathic tendencies. These tests will give degree of impairment in solid numerical figures.

From an orthomolecular point of view alcoholism can originate in four possible ways. The chronically depressed high-histamine patient is the hard-core drinker, the compulsive drinker, who commits very slow suicide. On the other hand, there's the low-histamine patient who gets so overstimulated periodically that a debauche is needed to deaden the stimulation. He's the one who goes on the weekend binge. Third, there's the alcoholic with cerebral allergy; he's allergic to the malt or yeast of the beverage he's chosen as a favorite food. In this case overindulgence occurs. In the fourth instance hypoglycemia may be a possible cause of alcoholism; the carbohydrate "alcohol" is substituted for the carbohydrate "sugar."

Nutrition has proved to be the most successful treatment of alcoholism (the patient must first join AA). Correction of nutritional deficiencies seems to have the most positive and lasting effect. Starting with a high protein diet, certain vitamins and minerals have been found to be highly useful in the treatment, such as niacin (vitamin B_3), which seems to inhibit the craving for alcohol. Therefore megadoses of this vitamin are indicated, plus pyridoxine (vitamin B_6) and sometimes vitamin E; this program at the Brain Bio Center has been successful in the treatment of more than 5,000 alcoholics. This nutritional approach has also proved to be effective in helping prevent acetaldehyde insult, which is a result of the oxidation of ethyl alcohol and is responsible for stupor of unconsciousness; the program also cuts down on the length of time of intoxication. In addition to these all-important vitamins the alcoholic needs all the other B vitamins, plentiful vitamin C and trace elements such as zinc, which are washed out of his system by the alcohol.

Three recurring problems can complicate the alcoholic's recovery: concurrent drug use, previously undetected hypoglycemia (several orthomolecular physicians believe alcoholism can even originate this way), and, third, perceptual distortions—of, for example, taste, hearing, vision, personal awareness, time and space. These perceptual disorders and the general characteristics of the alcoholic are similar to many experienced by the schizophrenic: the inappropriate affects of alcohol abuse include anxiety, hostile behavior, delusions and depression. The gradual development of serious depressive symptoms produces the high rate of suicidal attempts in alcoholics.

So—treatment depends on admitting the problem first, then an accurate diagnosis, a high protein diet and the use of nutrient therapy with emphasis on the B vitamins, C and zinc.

However, the doctor can't treat the alcoholic until he admits the problem and wants to get well. In other words, Alcoholics Anonymous or its equivalent is needed to begin with. Hospitalization alone won't cure him unless he agrees to ask others to help him stay away from alcohol. Those who themselves have traveled the long road to alcoholism and the harder road back are well equipped to understand the alcoholic and may spend long hours with him as he makes his slow psychological recovery. The first visit to an AA meeting may not much impress the alcoholic; sometimes it's only after greater damage has been done to his health that he finally agrees that his personality was not made for social drinking. The very spirit of AA, in which the goal is that of specifically helping others and oneself break the habit, may be the ultimate motivation that keeps the alcoholic dry. This is why it's imperative that the alcoholic become an active member of AA.

It appears, then, that with a sound program of attendance at AA meetings, solid nutritional treatment and proper counseling to solve whatever psychological problems exist, we can defeat this blight on our modern world.

10 🍁 Keeping Aging and Senility at Bay

Aging is a natural biological process; our biological clock starts ticking the moment we're born. Like Ponce de Leon we search endlessly for that elusive fountain of youth, and gradually our scientists are coming up with answers concerning causes of aging.

We do know that certain factors, such as poor diet, bad living habits and infection may lead to premature aging. The time to start thinking about aging and senility is while we're still young enough to avoid some of these pitfalls. The diseases of the aged are another matter, but fortunately modern science is making strides in their treatment and prevention.

Improper diet, causing a deficiency of essential minerals and vitamins, is probably the leading cause of premature aging. Furthermore, as we grow older and less active, our interest in food dwindles, and we're more apt to take the easy route and settle for the packaged, processed meal from the frozen food department—particularly if we're living alone. The resultant deficiencies, described in earlier chapters, take their toll.

Dr. Collin Dong, coauthor with Jane Banks of *The Arthritic's Cookbook*, recently visited the provinces of the

93

Caucasus in Russia. (Dr. Dong, incidentally, is a prime example himself of successful longevity attributable to diet.) He found the people in the Caucasus, great numbers of them, to be extremely longevous. Many of them were over 100, with some ranging up to 138—an almost unbelievable figure. Perhaps even more unbelievable is Dr. Dong's news that some of them were marrying and fathering children at 90. A geriatric institution in the republic of Georgia is making studies of the phenomenon and has come up with some interesting answers.

All these people, as well as similarly isolated groups in Pakistan and South America, live on a low cholesterol diet. They eat some fowl and fish, not much, and a little lamb. They consume little in the way of dairy products, mainly yoghurt and a little cheese and a few eggs. Their main source of food is vegetables, from which they derive a supply of zinc, chromium and vitamin C. (Perhaps their mountainous soil is not as depleted as ours.) The other factor contributing to their longevity is undoubtedly the enforced activity of maintaining life in a difficult environment. Compare these hardy people with the sad old people who fill our nursing homes and convalescent hospitals!

The confusion in older patients which results in senile behavior may be due to excess copper, aluminum and lead. Treatment with zinc and manganese has proved effective in alleviating this confusion; the combination of zinc with vitamin C has been found to mobilize the copper, etc., from the tissues.

Memory loss is for most of us the first symptom of approaching senility, with recall of recent events the first to go. We've found that this fiendish symptom of aging can be alleviated; memory can be restored through a combination of B_{12} (which, as we indicated earlier, must be injected, because it doesn't absorb well through the intestines), deanol, zinc and manganese, plus an adequate supply of vitamin C. Really, isn't it awful to forget your best friend's name on the point of introducing her? Educate your doctor to these findings, persuade him to their use. In any event, 15 mg of zinc gluconate night and morning plus at least 500 IU of vitamin E night and morning plus a chromium tablet will help delay membership in the geriatric set. In addition to supplements of these vitamins and minerals, the diet can lean heavily on foods rich in these elements. As previously mentioned, the confusion resulting from too much copper can be treated with these supplements of zinc and vitamin C. Why, then, can't all our geriatric patients have the benefits of supplement therapy suitable to their problems? Doesn't it follow that once these common conditions of old age have been dealt with, our old people will be able to live more normal lives, free of the disorientation and psychotic behavior so common now.

Certain other vitamins should be a part of the aging person's daily routine. Of these, perhaps vitamin E is the first in importance. Dr. Aloys L. Tappel, a biochemist at the University of California, says, "Aging is due to the process of oxidation." He thinks that aging is influenced by intercellular factors, by the effect of radiation on polyunsaturated lipids and the vitamin E available to protect them from excessive destruction. Dr. Tappel says that vitamin E is the most powerful antioxidant. As noted, wheat germ is our best source.

Dr. Tappel also thinks vitamin C can help to retard the aging process by improving cell structure; he also believes large amounts of C help your body protect itself against toxicity and stress, thereby prolonging life. Green peppers, brussels sprouts and citrus fruits are all good sources of C.

There is evidence that vitamin A helps to prevent premature aging and increases life expectancy. Fish liver oil is the richest source; others are carrots, tomatoes and green leafy vegetables.

In addition there should be a B complex supplement, a good tablespoonful of powdered lecithin and plenty of brewer's yeast. The latter is of the utmost importance; brewer's yeast is the source of the nucleic acids that are *the* key to staying young.

Cardiovascular disease is probably the most common ailment among older people, with hypertension and atherosclerosis the most common. Hypertension is of course high blood pressure, and atherosclerosis is a form of arteriosclerosis in which cholesterol and calcium are deposited in the arteries, thus hardening them and restricting the flow of blood. Although high cholesterol is possibly a contributing factor, adequate amounts of nutrients such as zinc, chromium and vitamin C can halt the condition's development in the first place.

There's also considerable evidence that harmful elements, particularly the metal contaminants from plumbing, may also predispose one to cardiovascular disease. However, we know that an adequate supply of zinc antagonizes and counteracts these dangerous elements.

Good nutrition promotes those other two keys to the secret of staying young: interests and exercise. Poor nutrition leads to apathy and insufficient energy to pursue interests or partake of exercise. However, with good nutrition and proper supplements older people can live happy, interesting lives. There's no reason why they shouldn't exercise to the limits of their strength, even indulging in such strenuous activities as tennis and golf. Swimming is of course an ideal exercise, as the body is supported in the water and pressure on the joints is very much reduced. Exercise seems to lead to other interests, as it tends to get one out and about; it tends to defeat the hold of the rocking chair.

The theory that one's ability to learn diminishes with age seems to be unfounded. Richard L. Sprott, a psychologist specializing in the study of behavior genetics, suggests it is time to reassess the view that learning depends on age. "Aging itself is not detrimental to learning ability and IQ," he said. "The factor instead is the health of the individual as he grows older." He added that advancing age usually brings failing health, with resultant loss of interest in learning. Actually, it's not the learning ability that's reduced—it's the performance level. Supporting this theory is the increasing number of college-enrolled oldsters, and the senior citizen programs included in many educational institutions become more popular all the time.

So—to the best of our knowledge, preventive nutrition is the best medicine for the aging body and mind. As one advances in age, there should be a reduction in saturated fat intake to prevent unnecessary arterial cholesterol deposits. Refined sugar and carbohydrates have been shown to be harmful to all ages; the elderly would do well to rely on the natural sugar content found in fresh fruits and vegetables.

The aging individual should also be aware of the dangers of alcohol. An occasional drink or two is all right, but alcohol in excess will certainly hasten bodily deterioration. The older patient should avoid strong alcoholic drinks and content himself with beer or wine, both of which are loaded with nutrients. In addition, if hard liquor is used, the adrenalin released may result in a wakeful night.

We can't prevent aging completely, any more than we can prevent death. However, with good nutrition, some exercise and an interesting occupation, we can certainly enjoy our lives longer. We may be designed to deteriorate with age, but with proper care we can retard the unwanted symptoms and keep on smiling.

The oldest man in the world, as far as we know, lives in the Caucasian mountains. He's 166 years old and he says, "There are two sources of long life: One is a gift of nature, and it is the pure air and clear water of the mountains, the fruit of the earth, peace, rest and the soft warm climate of the highlands. The second source is within us. He lives long who enjoys life and who bears no jealousy of others, whose heart harbors no malice or anger, who sings a lot and cries a little, who rises and retires with the sun, who likes to work and who knows how to rest."

11 🍁 Arthritis

Arthritis is another common disease whose exact cause remains unknown. We do know, however, that it affects upwards of forty million Americans in varying degrees, and in varying forms. Osteoarthritis is generally considered a deteriorative disease, afflicting in the main older people. Rheumatoid arthritis, on the other hand, is a very serious condition that can strike at any age, but occurs particularly in the young—even children.

Current available medical treatment of the disease offers aspirin, drugs and the steroid hormones, all of which have undesirable side effects. The anti-inflammatory effects of the drugs and hormones that are least harmful have a very limited lasting period of relief; the synthetic steroids such as hydrocortisone have a longer effect but have such undesirable side effects that they shouldn't be used except in an emergency. In other words, there doesn't seem to be any medical treatment at present which offers safe relief, let alone a "cure." So—one cannot help but agree with Dr. Roger Williams, former director of the Clayton Foundation Biochemical Institute at the University of Texas in Austin and discoverer of the B vitamin pantothenic acid, when he says, "When in doubt, try nutrition first."

Among the suspected causes of arthritis are bacterial infection such as repeated streptococcus throat, trauma and stress, exposure to heavy metals such as lead, and poor nutrition. The rheumatoid arthritic is always found to have a high level of serum copper and a low level of zinc, indicating that nutrition plays an important part in the disease.

Actually, a nutritional regimen has proved to be the most successful method of treating arthritis. Dr. Collin Dong states that if we give the body only what it needs for proper nutrition, eliminating certain foods he has found to be undesirable for the arthritic, we can bring about long-term, probably permanent, relief. A balance of protein to replace the cells, vegetables for the minerals and vitamins and carbohydrates for energy is his dietary regimen. He eliminates meat completely, also all dairy products and all fruits. (The first two because of bacterial and allergy factors, the last to eliminate all acids.) Obviously, this leaves a very simple diet of fish, white meat of chicken, vegetables, grains and nuts. His remarkable success with thousands and thousands of followers of this regimen bears witness to its efficacy.

In addition, Dr. Williams, in his book *Nutrition Against Disease,* suggests some supplements that have been found to help the arthritic. His findings indicate that many sufferers are deficient in certain vitamins and minerals. Zinc, as we've mentioned, is a necessary supplement, and it can be supplied, along with needed manganese, by a product called Ziman (more about which in Chapter 12). This will antagonize the arthritic's high copper and raise his zinc level. Also needed are supplements of niacin, pantothenic acid, folic acid and pyridoxine (B_6).

Sulfur is also necessary for combating copper, and because egg yolks are among the few food sources of this element, it follows that eggs should occupy an important place in the arthritic's diet. In fact, we strongly recommend two a day, as we already have for a general diet (oddly enough, the arthritic often avoids eggs). However, if one's cholesterol count doesn't allow eggs, elemental sulfur can be supplied at the level of 200 mg a day. Add a plentiful supply of vitamin C to mobilize heavy metals, at least 1000 mg night and morning, and ten brewer's yeast tablets twice a day. (As noted earlier these tablets should be started at the level of two or three and gradually increased to avoid gastric discomfort.)

Often the severely afflicted sufferer from rheumatoid arthritis will be thin and run-down, poorly nourished, because of lack of appetite. The enforced inactivity and pain contribute to this, and conscious effort must be made to provide the good, balanced nutrition the arthritic so sorely needs.

Protein is of the utmost importance, both because of its role in the formation of new cells and tissues and its resistance to disease. Seafood offers us a complete protein, with additional gifts from the sea in the form of valuable elements. Potatoes, green peppers, cabbage, leafy greens contain vitamins and minerals necessary to the arthritic, as do many other vegetables. Use as many raw vegetables as possible because of the vitamin and mineral loss in cooking.

Use polyunsaturated oils such as safflower oil in place of other fats whenever possible. Avoid additives like the plague, particularly monosodium glutamate; the arthritic is particularly sensitive to these chemicals.

This regimen may seem restricting, but only the arthritic sufferer can recognize that anything is worthwhile if it alleviates the pain. Actually, it's a very healthy, tasty way to eat, and when combined with suggested supplements, this diet will more than likely bring about great improvement in an arthritic's condition.

12 🍁 Something for Everyone

The Brain Bio Center treats "normal" people and patients from a metabolic-nutritional viewpoint. This book should have convinced you that proper diet is essential to the health of all of us; selection of the right foods is within everyone's reach, and probably more economical than the junk foods. The ideal, of course, is a nutritional program supervised by the family physician. If only doctors were urged to participate more in nutritional guidance; if only they'd become more interested in nutrition!

To recapitulate, the diet should contain as much as possible of the following foods: whole grains and whole grain bread, fresh or dried fruits, vegetables, wheat germ, sprouted seeds, legumes (such as lentils, peas, beans), nuts, cheese, eggs, milk, brewer's yeast, sea food, poultry, organ meats and lean meats. The diet should include at least one tablespoon of safflower oil a day; safflower oil can replace butter and margarine in many ways, in cooking included. It should of course be used as the salad oil and can be mixed with the wheat germ as a morning cereal with milk and fruit. Skimmed milk powder can be used in making sauces; it has many low-calorie uses. Eggs should be eaten daily if the cholesterol allows; those allergic to eggs can usually tolerate the yolk. The recipes that make up Part Two are intended as examples of the sort of fare that can be enjoyed while promoting good health.

The doctor should not prescribe, and the patient should not take, commercial *vitamins plus minerals.* These are usually supplemented with copper, which, as we have made clear, we get in excess from our copper plumbing. We recommend bottled water if the house water supply is high in copper or otherwise undesirable (brass-activated carbon filters may actually add even more copper to drinking water). Aluminum may be high in city waters because aluminum sulfate is used to clarify water.

We have compiled a chart of specific products that are recommended. Most good pharmacies now carry these items, but if necessary they can be ordered by mail from the suggested suppliers. The following preparations are those most frequently needed according to age.

INFANTS MAY NEED:

Pyri-Zinc liquid (in dropping bottles)
Contains 100 mgm B_6/ml 50 mgm zinc gluconate/ml (6.25 mgm zinc)

Willner Chemists
330 Lexington Ave.
New York, N.Y. 10016

or

B_6 and zinc drops (60 ml)

Bronson Pharmaceuticals
4526 Rinetti Lane
La Canada, Calif. 91011

For newborn infants the starting dose may be one drop per day.

CHILDREN:

The zinc and B_6 liquid preparations listed above can also be used for children but at a correspondingly greater dosage. Pleasant dream recall is normal and B_6 will cause pleasant dreams that can be remembered in the morning.

White spots on the fingernails are a sign of zinc deficiency, and zinc gluconate should be given—15 mgm morning and evening. Zinc and vitamin C, 1 to 2 gr per day, may be needed to lower the lead level of children who live along our arterial highways. They are exposed to lead pollution from automobile exhaust.

TEENAGERS:

Vitamin C, 2 gr/day
B_6 (enough for dream recall)
Ziman Fortified capsules (a
source of zinc and
manganese)

Willner Chemists
New York, N.Y.

or

Vicon Plus, 1 capsule/day

Meyer Laboratories
Ft. Lauderdale, Fla.
33309

Iodized salt or 1 kelp tablet daily

The hormones at puberty make great demands for adequate mineral intake. These demands are not met by the usual teenage diet of jiffy foods, nor are they met by standard vitamins plus minerals high in copper. Acne, amenorrhea and delayed puberty can result from zinc deficiency. Also, girls who eat very little meat should have one Mol-Iron tablet a day. This provides iron and the essential trace element molybdenum, which may help to control excess bone growth at puberty.

ADULTS:

Vicon Plus or Ziman Fortified, 1 capsule/day (The manganese in these products may elevate blood pressure in certain individuals, in which case zinc alone, 15 to 30 mgm night and morning, should be taken. Or Vicon C or Zimag C may be substituted.)

Brewer's yeast, 3 tablets morning and night (for the chromium containing glucose tolerance factor.)

Vitamin C, 2 gr/day (2,500 mgm tablets morning and night)

Dolomite, if not drinking milk

Vitamin A, 25,000 IU/day

Vitamin E, 400 IU/day

Safflower oil, 1 tbs/day

Low salt diet, using Morton's Salt Substitute for its potassium

GERIATRICS:

In addition to needing natural foods, vitamins C, E and A, zinc, B_6, brewer's yeast, and safflower oil, the senior citizens have special needs:

Calcium dolomite, 2 tablets morning and night

Magnesium oxide, 300 mgm, 2 tablets morning and night

Vitamin B_{12}, 100 mcg/day

Folic acid, 0.4 mgm/day

Inositol, 650 mgm/day

Lecithin, 700 mgm morning and night

With these supplements to a natural food diet the elderly can combat the disabilities of age. A preventive program is far more effective than the use of drugs against symptoms.

13 🍁 Food Sources of Vitamins and Minerals

VITAMIN A

Mainly:
Cod liver oil
Fish and animal livers

Present in:
Egg yolk
Butter
Margarine
Milk, cream, milk
   products
Apricots, fresh and dried
Carrots, particularly
   dehydrated
Tomatoes

Endive
Parsley
Peaches, fresh and dried
Spinach
Dandelion greens
Collard greens
Kale
Mustard greens
Sweet potatoes,
   particularly dehydrated
Turnip greens
Watercress
Winter squash

VITAMIN B₁

Mainly:
Brewer's yeast

Soybeans
Lean pork

Present in:
Wheat, wheat bran
Lentils
Beef heart
Lima beans, dried
Barley
Cashew nuts
Walnuts
Cornmeal

Egg yolk
Ham (eat fresh ham or
    plain smoked ham only)
Beef kidney
Oatmeal
Peanuts, peanut butter
Peas, particularly split
Pecans

VITAMIN B$_2$

Mainly:
Brewer's yeast
Whey
Liver
Kidney

Present in:
Milk, dried whole and
    skim
Wheat germ
Whole wheat flour
Dried beans

Beef and lamb heart
Hickory nuts
Eggs
Spinach
Crabmeat
Wheat bran
Oysters
Turnip greens
Collard greens
Cheddar cheese
Roquefort cheese
Swiss cheese

VITAMIN B$_3$

Mainly:
Brewer's yeast
Wheat bran

Present in:
Peanuts, peanut butter

Liver
Beef kidney
Chicken
Beef heart
Fish
Turkey

Veal
Beef
Brown rice
Lamb

Buckwheat
Pork
Mushrooms

VITAMIN B$_6$

Mainly:
Brewer's yeast
Milk
Unprocessed wheat

Present in:
Beef liver
Lima beans

Bananas
Cabbage
Molasses
Peas, dried
Peanuts
Pork loin
Wheat germ
Sweet potatoes
Beef, round

VITAMIN B$_{12}$

Mainly:
Liver

Present in:
Egg yolk
Cheese

VITAMIN C

Mainly:
Pimentos
Green peppers
Mustard greens
Brussels sprouts
Turnip greens
Citrus fruits

Present in:
Broccoli
Guavas
Kale
Honeydew melon
Cantaloupe
Collard greens

Dandelion greens
Parsley
Peas
Persimmon
Raspberries, particularly
   black
Watercress
Pears

Strawberries
Tomatoes
Spinach
Lima beans
Cabbage
Pineapple
Currants
Swiss chard

VITAMIN D

Mainly:
Fortified milk

Present in:
Butter
Fish
Egg yolk
Liver

VITAMIN E

Mainly:
Wheat germ oil
Peanut oil
Cottonseed oil

Present in:
Corn oil
Soybean oil
Margarine
Sweet potatoes
Navy beans

Beef liver
Cornmeal
Eggs
Oatmeal
Brown rice
Turnip greens
Spinach
Other leafy green
   vegetables
Rabbit
Squirrel

INOSITOL

Mainly:
Beef heart
Beef liver

Present in:
Yeast
Peanuts
Wheat germ

Barley
Whole wheat
Cantaloupe
Grapefruit
Molasses
Cabbage
Peas
Oranges

ZINC

Mainly:
Atlantic oysters
Herring
Sunflower seeds

Present in:
Wheat bran
Wheat germ
Oatmeal
Milk
Nuts
Liver, particularly pork
Broccoli
Mushrooms

Brewer's yeast
Onions
Peanut butter
Eggs
Corn
Unpolished rice
Whole wheat and rye
Beef
Chicken thigh and breast
Peas
Carrots
Clams
Lamb

IRON

Mainly:
Organ meats
Wheat germ

Present in:
Lean meat
Eggs

Legumes, particularly
  lentils
Dried fruits
Shellfish
Whole grain cereals or
  bread

Sunflower seeds
Deep-green leafy
  vegetables
Blackstrap molasses

MANGANESE

Mainly:
Bran
Corn germ
Walnuts

Present in:
Buckwheat
Cloves
Dried peas
Dried beans
Blueberries
Chestnuts

Peanuts
Pecans
Cardamom seeds
Ginger
Spinach
Tea leaves
Coffee beans
Wheat
Corn
Rice
Oats

SULFUR

Mainly:
Egg yolks

Present in:
Beef
Bran
Egg whites
Brussels sprouts
Cabbage
Dried peas and beans

Oysters
Nuts
Clams
Fish
Poultry
Cheese
Garlic
Onions
Watercress

SELENIUM

Mainly:
Brewer's yeast
Liver
Garlic
Eggs

Present in:
Cheese
Wheat germ

Tuna
Herring
Brown rice
Whole wheat
Bran
Cabbage
Onions
Broccoli
Tomatoes

CALCIUM

Mainly:
Milk (skimmed as good as
   whole)
Bone meal
Cheese

Present in:
Kale
Mustard greens
Turnip greens
Parsley
Watercress
Dandelion greens

MAGNESIUM

Mainly:
Milk
Nuts
Whole grains

Present in:
Green vegetables
Seafoods

POTASSIUM

Mainly:
Navy beans, dried
Spinach
Nuts, particularly peanuts
Lima beans
Wheat germ

Present in:
Broccoli
Cauliflower
Celery
Carrots
Potatoes
Beets
Wheat
Oats
Apricots
Bananas
Corn
Beef
Codfish
Liver
Lamb
Turkey
Citrus juices

MOLYBDENUM

Mainly:
Buckwheat grain
   (unprocessed)
Lima beans

Present in:
Wheat germ
Oats
Soybeans
Lentils
Sunflower seeds
Liver

CHROMIUM

Mainly:
Brewer's yeast

Present in:
Liver
Beef
Whole grains
   (unprocessed)
Beets
Mushrooms
Beer
Peanuts
Dried beans
Cheese

Part Two ❧ Recipes

These recipes have been devised by Jane Banks to utilize as much as possible of those foods containing the minerals and vitamins we need. Some, as we have pointed out, are more valuable than others in treating certain conditions; all are sources of some of the essential nutrients.

As mentioned previously, fresh produce is important. Grow your own if you can; in any event, don't shop once a week—shop every day if possible. Remember to avoid lead, copper and aluminum in your cooking utensils— avoid even aluminum foil! Cook your fresh vegetables briefly in as little water as possible; save the water for use in soups or stews. Don't peel your vegetables and fruits except when necessary, as you're throwing away valuable nutrients and fiber. Use Morton's Salt Substitute, not only to avoid salt but to benefit from its potassium content.

Most of the recipes serve four, except where obviously otherwise.

Soups

GAZPACHO

  ½ tbs parsley, minced
  ½ tsp tarragon, minced (fresh if possible)
  ½ cucumber, peeled and seeded
  ½ green pepper, seeded and chopped
  4 green onions (scallions), chopped
  1 lb tomatoes, peeled, seeded and chopped
  4 tbs safflower oil
  ½ tsp lemon juice
  1 tbs tomato paste
     Salt
  4 cups chicken broth
     Cucumber and green pepper for garnish

Crush parsley and tarragon to a paste and add to cucumber and green pepper. Puree in blender, then add green onions, tomatoes, oil, lemon juice, tomato paste and salt to taste. Mix well with broth, chill at least two hours, serve garnished with chopped green pepper and cucumber.

COCK-A-LEEKIE

 1 bunch leeks
 1 onion, chopped
 3 stalks celery, chopped
 3 tbs safflower oil
 1 lb potatoes, diced
 2 cups chicken stock
    Milk
    Salt

Sauté leeks, onion and celery in the oil till soft. Add the potatoes and stock and simmer for about an hour and a half. Put through blender, food processor or sieve. Before serving add enough milk to make a thick, creamy soup, salt to taste, and heat well.

CIOPPINO
(contains the B vitamins, D, zinc, iron, sulfur, magnesium)

 2 medium onions, chopped
 5 tbs safflower oil
 4 cloves garlic, crushed
    Handful of parsley, chopped
 ¼ cup dry white wine
 2 cans whole tomatoes, chopped
 2 cans tomato paste
 ¼ tsp thyme
    Salt
 1 small lobster
 2 lb uncooked fish (sea bass, red snapper or cod) cut in bite size

8 large uncooked shrimp
12 raw clams

Sauté onions in the oil, add garlic and parsley and cook, stirring. Add wine, tomatoes with juice from cans, tomato paste, thyme and salt to taste. Add the lobster, simmer covered for 15 minutes, then add fish, shrimp and clams and cook covered till clams open.

NAVY BEAN SOUP
(*rich in potassium and manganese*)

1 lb dried white navy beans
2 qt water
½ cup onion, chopped
¼ cup green pepper, chopped
2 stalks celery, chopped
½ tbs parsley, minced
2 cloves garlic, crushed
1 ham bone
Large pinch cayenne
Large pinch crushed red peppers
Several pinches thyme
Several pinches basil
1 bay leaf, crushed
Salt substitute to taste

Soak beans overnight. Drain and put in a heavy pot with rest of ingredients. Simmer for three hours or till beans are very soft. Remove the ham bone and any meat and strain the soup through a coarse sieve. Add about a cup of the beans from the sieve to the soup, heat well and serve.

OYSTER STEW
(rich in zinc)

> 1 onion, chopped
> 2 tbs safflower oil
> 2 tbs whole wheat flour
> 1½ cups oyster liquid
> 2 cups oysters removed from shells (canned can
>   be used if fresh are unavailable)
>   Salt

Cook the onion in the oil, add the flour and stir till browned. Turn heat low and add the oyster liquid carefully, stirring till smooth. Add the oysters, cook till they curl, season to taste and serve immediately.

PEANUT BUTTER SOUP
(rich in B vitamins)

> 2 tbs onion, minced
> 1 tbs margarine
> 1 tbs safflower oil
> 1 tbs whole wheat flour
> 1 qt chicken stock
> 1 cup unadulterated peanut butter
> 1 cup milk
>   Salt to taste
>   Madeira wine (optional)

Sauté onion in margarine and oil. Stir in flour, add small amount of stock and stir till smooth. Add peanut butter and rest of stock, stir till smooth. Add milk. A little

Madeira wine, added just before serving, is a fine extra touch.

SPLIT PEA SOUP

½   lb split peas
1½ qt water
1   small ham bone
¼   cup celery, chopped fine
1   onion, chopped
    Salt substitute

Soak the peas in the water overnight. Drain and combine all other ingredients and cook till peas are very well done, very soft.

GARLIC SOUP

6   large garlic cloves, peeled
5   cups water
1   tbs Vegex (liquid Vegex in jar, available health food stores)
4   slices French bread
¼   cup margarine
    Grated Parmesan cheese
    Sherry

Simmer the garlic in the water and Vegex until the garlic is very soft—about a half-hour. Toast bread on one side, remove garlic from soup and mix with margarine, mashing well. Spread on bread, sprinkle with cheese, broil a few minutes. Place a piece of toast in each bowl and pour soup over, adding a dash of sherry to each bowl.

LENTIL SOUP
(potassium and molybdenum in the lentils, sulfur in the onions, vitamins in all the vegetables)

> 1   cup lentils
> ½   cup celery, chopped fine
> ¼   cup onion, chopped fine
> ¼   cup carrots, chopped fine
> 1   qt water
>   Salt to taste

Wash the lentils. (Use the kind that doesn't require soaking, such as Golden Grain brand.) Simmer all ingredients together for about two hours.

CREAM OF VEGETABLE SOUP
(This version of the old standby has us cook the vegetables and then combine them with a wheat-rich sauce, thus giving us a wide variety of nutrients—from the C in the parsley to the zinc in the corn.)

> ¼   cup onion, coarsely chopped
> ¼   cup celery, chopped
> ¼   cup corn
> ¼   cup mushrooms, sliced
> ¼   cup green pepper, chopped
> ½   cup water
> 3   tbs safflower oil
> 4   tbs whole wheat flour
> 3   cups milk (or chicken stock), heated
>   Salt to taste

Pinch each of thyme, marjoram and dill weed
Parsley or watercress for garnish

Sauté all the vegetables in a teaspoon of the oil for five minutes. Add the water, cover and steam till tender. Blend the flour with the remaining oil in another pan, and cook, stirring, over low heat for about four minutes. Gradually add the heated milk or stock, and simmer for a few minutes. Add the vegetables and seasonings, simmer for another ten minutes and serve either as is or smoothed in the blender. Garnish with minced parsley or watercress.

CLAM CHOWDER
(*good source of zinc*)

> 1 onion, diced
> 1 carrot, diced
> 2 stalks celery, chopped
> 2 tbs safflower oil
> 2 cups clam juice
> Good pinch thyme
> 1 cup rich milk
> 1 pt shucked clams (or 1 can razorback clams), chopped
> Salt to taste
> 1 tbs chopped parsley

Sauté the onion, carrot and celery in the oil till onion is transparent. Add the clam juice and thyme and simmer about ten minutes or till vegetables are done. Add the milk, clams and salt and heat thoroughly but do not boil. Serve at once generously sprinkled with parsley.

VEGETARIAN MINESTRONE
(another soup that's a meal in itself with some crusty whole wheat bread)

¾ cup dried kidney beans
Water
2 cloves garlic, crushed
½ large onion, chopped
1½ tbs olive oil
1½ tbs safflower oil
2 medium potatoes, cut in chunks without peeling
1 carrot, sliced
½ cup string beans, cut in pieces
3 zucchini, sliced
2 leeks, sliced (white part only)
¼ cup parsley, chopped
1 tsp basil
½ tsp oregano
Pinch marjoram
Pinch celery seeds
Salt
¼ head cabbage, sliced thin
¼ cup unpolished rice
3 tomatoes, cut in wedges
2 tbs margarine
½ cup Parmesan cheese, grated

Soak the beans overnight in water to cover. Drain and put into a pot with 2 quarts of water. Simmer for 1½ hours. Add the garlic, onion and both oils. Add the potatoes, carrot, beans, zucchini, and leeks, half the parsley, the seasonings and salt to taste and simmer again for 45 minutes. Add the cabbage and rice and simmer another 20 minutes. About five minutes before serving add the tomatoes, margarine, cheese and the rest of the parsley.

POT AU FEU
(provides B₆, zinc, C, sulfur and potassium, among other nutrients)

   1 lb beef round, trimmed of all fat and cut in cubes
1½ tbs safflower oil
1½ qt water
   2 bay leaves, crushed
   1 tsp marjoram
½ tsp thyme
   6 cloves
   2 tbs parsley
      Salt to taste
½ cup onion, chopped
½ cup celery, including leaves, chopped
½ cup carrots, chopped
   4 cabbage wedges
   4 potatoes, quartered

Brown the beef in the oil and add the water and seasonings. Bring to a boil, cover and simmer for three hours. Remove meat from stock and strain. Return meat to stock, add all the vegetables and simmer 45 minutes. The meat and vegetables can be served on a plate with the stock in a bowl—or all together as a soup.

Salads

TOSSED GREEN SALAD

 Fresh salad greens such as romaine, Bibb, endive
¼ cup olive oil
¼ cup safflower oil
¼ cup, skimpy, of red wine vinegar
¼ tsp dill weed
 Vegesalt to taste
 Few drops Worcestershire sauce
1 clove garlic, crushed (optional)

Wash the greens and dry them well and tear them into reasonably sized pieces. Mix the dressing ingredients thoroughly, pour over greens and toss.

GREEK SALAD
(C in the peppers, zinc in the mushrooms)

1 head iceberg lettuce
 Safflower oil seasoned with a little olive oil
 Lemon juice
 Vegesalt

    Oregano
1 cucumber, sliced, not peeled
1 lb feta cheese
½ lb fresh mushrooms, sliced
1 box cherry tomatoes, each cut in half
¼ lb black olives (Greek if possible)
¼ lb green olives (Greek if possible)
1 green pepper, seeded and sliced thin

Line an oval platter with the crisp outer leaves of the lettuce. Tear the rest into small pieces and toss with oil, lemon juice, salt to taste and oregano. Arrange pieces carefully on the platter. Place the cucumber slices around the rim of the platter and then make a ring of cheese inside it, then a ring of mushrooms, and alternate all the rest. Finish with a mound of the black olives and cherry tomatoes in the center. Do not toss! It should make a beautiful display. Serve with extra dressing in a small pitcher.

SPINACH SALAD
(contains both A and E, as well as potassium and manganese)

1 bunch fresh small-leaved spinach, well washed
3 green onions, sliced thin
2 heaping tbs broken walnut pieces
    Dressing as for Tossed Green Salad, using about half

Dry the spinach well, using only the leaves and tearing any large ones into smaller pieces. Toss all ingredients together. Imitation bacon bits add greatly if you can find them without additives.

LIMA BEAN SALAD
(Lima beans are rich in B_1, B_6, potassium and molybdenum.)

    1 cup large dried lima beans
    ¾ qt water
    ¼ cup mixed olive and safflower oil
    ⅛ cup red wine vinegar
       Vegesalt

Simmer the beans in the water for an hour, then drain, keeping the liquid. Boil the liquid vigorously in a shallow pan until thickened. Add the other ingredients to ⅓ cup of the thickened liquid while still warm, pour over the beans and refrigerate for 2 or 3 hours. Stir gently before serving.

LENTIL AND LEEK SALAD
(a high protein salad with B_1 and molybdenum)

    4 leeks, washed
    ½ cup lentils, washed
       Small stalk celery, chopped fine
    ½ small onion, chopped fine
       Small clove garlic, crushed

Cut the tops from the leeks and braise them gently, then drain and set aside. Cover the lentils with 1½ cups hot water, add celery, onion and garlic and simmer for about an hour or till tender. When lentils and leeks are room temperature, cut the leek stalks in half and lay on a lettuce leaf. Place a mound of lentils next to the leeks, and pour over all the following dressing:

¼ cup parsley, finely chopped
¼ onion, finely chopped
½ tsp prepared mustard
  Salt to taste
1 tbs olive oil
1 tbs safflower oil
1½ tbs lemon juice

Mix the parsley, onion, mustard and salt together, then add the mixed oils gradually while stirring. When the mixture thickens add the lemon juice, beating thoroughly.

BROCCOLI SALAD WITH CHEESE
(C and selenium in the broccoli, as well as zinc; selenium and sulfur in the eggs and cheese)

1 lb broccoli
3 tbs safflower oil
2½ tbs lemon juice
1½ tbs green onions, minced
½ tsp garlic salt or Vegesalt
½ tsp dry mustard
  Lettuce leaves
2 hard-boiled eggs, chopped
2½ tbs crumbled blue cheese
4 radishes, sliced

Wash and trim broccoli, peeling outer layers of stalks. Cook in boiling water to cover till just tender, drain and chill. Mix the oil, lemon juice, green onion, salt and mustard and let stand for some time. An hour before serving, arrange the broccoli on lettuce leaves, sprinkle with the egg and blue cheese and pour the dressing over all. Garnish with the sliced radishes.

MIXED VEGETABLE SALAD

     1 large potato, peeled
     2 medium carrots, peeled
     ½ cup green beans, frenched
     ½ cup fresh peas, shelled
     ¼ head cauliflower
     ½ cucumber, peeled and seeded
        Dressing as for Tossed Green Salad
        Parsley, chopped
     1 tbs capers

Cut the potatoes and carrots into ¾-inch cubes; cook
them in boiling water with the beans and peas slightly
more than five minutes. Break up the cauliflower into
small flowerets and cook carefully in boiling water till
just barely tender. Cube the cucumber, combine the vegetables and toss with the dressing as for Tossed Green
Salad. Chill, heap it on a serving dish and garnish with
the parsley and capers.

NORMANDY SALAD

        Crisp butter lettuce
        Red cabbage, shredded
        Farmer's cheese, crumbled
        Walnuts
        Oil
        Vinegar
        Salt

Mix all together in proportion to your taste—with the
red cabbage adding only a bit of crunchy flavor and color.
Dress with oil and vinegar, and salt to taste.

ORGANIC SALAD

    2 cups cabbage, shredded
1½ cups fresh bean sprouts
    1 cup carrots, shredded
  ½ cup alfalfa sprouts

Mix all together and dress with:

    1 tbs safflower oil
    1 tbs lemon juice
  ½ tbs coriander
  ½ tbs dried green onion
      Small clove garlic, crushed
      Salt to taste

Blend all ingredients. This dressing keeps well in the refrigerator for two or three days.

PERFECT MAYONNAISE

  1 egg
  1 egg yolk
  3 tbs lemon juice
  1 cup safflower oil
    Salt to taste

Place the egg and egg yolk in a food processor or blender. Add 1 tbs of the lemon juice and 1 tsp of the oil. Turn the machine on and immediately begin adding the oil in a thin threadlike stream. When it begins to thicken you can add faster. When all the oil is used, add the rest of the lemon juice and the salt. Turn off the machine as soon as all ingredients are blended.

 **Seafood**

FRIED OYSTERS
(our richest source of zinc)

Wash 24 shelled oysters to remove sand. Shake in a bag with a little whole wheat flour to coat evenly. Fry in 2 inches of hot safflower oil for about 1½ minutes; drain on paper towels. Divide evenly on 4 slices of toast and sprinkle generously with chopped parsley.

HERRING WITH DILL SAUCE
(Herring is another prime source of zinc.)

      4 fresh herring
         Salt to taste
     ½ cup mustard
     ½ cup safflower oil
      2 tbs wine vinegar
         Juice of ½ lemon
     ½ cup fresh dill, chopped (or 4 tbs dried dill weed)

Remove the skin and fillet the herring (or get the fish man to do it). Sprinkle with salt. Beat together the mustard and oil, and gradually add the vinegar. Add the lemon and dill and pour over the herring. Place, covered tightly, in the refrigerator for 3 or 4 days until well marinated.

BAKED FISH WITH MUSHROOMS

    1   whole fish, about 3 lb (lingcod, sea bass, flounder
          —any small fish)
    ⅓   cup whole wheat flour
    1   tsp Morton's Salt Substitute
        Pinch cayenne
    ⅛   tsp basil
    2   tbs margarine
    ⅓   lb mushrooms, sliced
    4   small whole potatoes
    ¾   cup clam juice
    ½   cup dry white wine

Have fish cleaned, with head and backbone removed. Wipe with a damp cloth and make 4 two-inch cuts on one side of fish. Blend together the flour, salt substitute, cayenne and basil. Sprinkle fish with the mixture and lay it in a shallow baking dish. With a teaspoon push the margarine into the cuts in the fish and bake in a 350° oven. At the end of a half-hour arrange the mushrooms and potatoes around the fish and continue cooking for another half-hour, basting with the clam juice and wine. Serve on a preheated platter with mushrooms and potatoes arranged around the fish and the pan liquid poured over.

FISH SALAD

3 cups flaked fish (any firm fish that flakes easily, even canned tuna packed in spring water)
2 stalks celery, minced
½ green pepper, seeded and minced
4 hard-boiled eggs, chopped coarsely
½ cup mayonnaise
   Pinch cayenne
¼ tsp dry mustard
   Crisp lettuce leaves
2 tomatoes, quartered

Mix the fish with the celery, green pepper and chopped eggs, being careful not to mash the fish flakes. Carefully fold in the mayonnaise, to which has been added the cayenne and mustard. Serve on lettuce garnished with the tomato quarters.

LINGUINE WITH CLAM SAUCE

2 onions, minced
2 cloves garlic, crushed
3 tbs safflower oil
   Juice from canned clams
¼ cup parsley, minced
1 can whole baby clams
12 fresh clams, unopened
1 8-oz box whole wheat linguine
   Parmesan cheese, grated

Sauté the onions and garlic in the oil till transparent, taking care not to burn the garlic. Add the juice from the canned clams and simmer for a half-hour or more. Add the parsley and simmer for about ten minutes; just before serving add the canned clams and lay the fresh clams on top. Cover tightly and simmer for 8 minutes or until clams open. Serve over the linguine, which has been boiled according to the directions on the package. Serve accompanied by a generous bowl of grated Parmesan.

TUNA CASSEROLE
(Tuna is a good source of selenium.)

    2 cans solid white tuna (albacore) packed in spring
         water
    6 soda crackers, crushed
    1 cup milk
    2 eggs
    1 cup creamed cottage cheese
    ¼ cup celery, chopped
    ½ cup onion, minced
    1 tbs lemon juice
    2 tsps Worcestershire sauce
       Pinch cayenne
       Salt to taste
       Parmesan cheese, grated

Flake the tuna in a bowl; add the crushed crackers and the milk. Beat the eggs well and add them with the cottage cheese. Gently add all the rest of the ingredients except the Parmesan. Pour into a casserole and sprinkle top with Parmesan. Bake for 30 minutes at 350°.

BROILED PRAWNS
(Shellfish contain, among other nutrients, iron and sulfur.)

    12 prawns
     3 tbs parsley, chopped
     2 cloves garlic, crushed
     1 tbs basil
     1 cup mixed safflower and olive oil

Prawns are so expensive now that they must be treated as a precious delicacy. Shell them, removing the vein. Mix all the other ingredients and marinate the prawns overnight in the mixture, tightly covered and refrigerated. Place them in a shallow pan and pour the marinade over them; broil under a hot flame for 6 or 7 minutes. Serve the remaining marinade as a sauce.

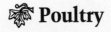 **Poultry**

CHICKEN BREASTS WITH MUSHROOMS
(There's zinc in those mushrooms!)

  3 tbs safflower oil
  4 chicken breasts
12 large mushrooms, peeled and sliced
  2 tsps chopped green onions
½ cup chicken bouillon
  2 tbs safflower margarine
  1 tsp parsley, minced
  1 tsp fresh tarragon, chopped (½ tsp dried)

Heat the oil in a skillet, add the chicken breasts, cover and cook briskly for about ten minutes, shaking and rolling the pan from time to time. Add the mushrooms and continue cooking for another ten minutes. Add the green onions, stirring till sautéed; add the bouillon and simmer for a few minutes, stirring constantly. Dot with margarine. Serve sprinkled with parsley and tarragon. Vitamin- and mineral-rich lima beans make a good accompaniment.

CHICKENBURGERS FOR TWO

    1 skinned and boned chicken breast, uncooked
    1 stalk celery
    1 tsp Worcestershire sauce
    1 egg yolk
    1 tbs safflower oil

Chop the raw chicken and the celery in a blender, or
better still, a food processor. Add the egg yolk and
Worcestershire, form into two patties and sauté in the oil
for just 3 minutes on each side.

WHEAT GERM CHICKEN ROLLS

    ½ cup toasted wheat germ
    ¼ cup green onions, chopped
    ½ tsp basil, crushed
    1 clove garlic, crushed
    ¼ cup melted margarine
    2 tbs whole wheat flour
    2 tsp chicken stock
    1 cup milk
    4 half chicken breasts, skinned and boned
    1 tbs safflower oil

Mix wheat germ, onion, basil and garlic into the melted
margarine. Make a sauce by combining the flour with the
chicken stock, simmer for a few minutes and gradually
add the milk. When smooth add one tablespoon of sauce
to the wheat germ mixture. Place the chicken breasts
between wax paper and flatten them with a mallet. Di-

vide the wheat germ mixture among the four chicken breasts, placing it in the center of each. Roll breasts around stuffing, fasten with toothpicks and brown in the oil. When nicely browned, place carefully in a small baking dish and cover with the sauce and a tight lid. Bake in a 400° oven for 45 minutes.

CHICKEN WINGS

  2 lb chicken wing "drumettes" (packaged at the market)
  ⅓ cup soy sauce
  ⅓ cup water
  2 tbs sugar
  1 tbs dry sherry
  2 slices ginger root
    Few cloves of star anise

Put all the ingredients in a saucepan or dutch oven. Bring to a boil and simmer covered for 20 minutes, stirring occasionally. Simmer wings without the cover until only about a half-cup of liquid remains. Spoon this remaining liquid over the wings and serve hot or cold. If hot they should be accompanied by rice. Cold they make a very good picnic item.

CHICKEN AND ALMOND SANDWICHES
(delicious way to use up leftover chicken)

  1 cup chicken, chopped rather fine
  1 cup almonds, chopped
  6 tbs mayonnaise
  8 slices whole wheat bread spread with margarine

Combine the first three and make four sandwiches.

CHICKEN IN YOGHURT

2½ lb chicken breasts, thighs and legs
3   tbs lemon juice
     Salt
¼   cup plain yoghurt
½   onion, chopped
1   clove garlic, crushed
1   green hot chili pepper
1   tsp ginger root, minced

Skin the chicken pieces and cut the whole breasts into 4 pieces. Cut some diagonal slits on the meaty portion of the pieces. Arrange the chicken in one layer in a shallow glass pan and rub each piece with lemon juice and salt, covering thoroughly. Let stand for 15 or 20 minutes. Meanwhile, combine the rest of the ingredients in a blender or food processor and run till the mixture becomes a smooth paste. Pour it over the chicken, rub it in well and let the chicken marinate in the refrigerator, covered tightly, overnight. Bake the chicken in one layer in a very hot oven, 500°, for 15 minutes. Remove the breast pieces, keep them warm, and continue cooking the rest of the chicken for about 10 minutes more.

CHICKEN PROVENÇAL

1   3-lb chicken, cut into serving pieces
     Whole wheat flour for dredging
4   tbs safflower oil mixed with 1 tbs olive oil
1   small red pepper, sliced
1   small green pepper, sliced

2 cloves garlic, crushed
½ cup dry red wine
4 tomatoes, peeled, seeded and chopped
⅔ cup green ripe olives
¼ tsp thyme
¼ tsp basil
¼ tsp marjoram

Shake the chicken pieces in a paper bag containing a little whole wheat flour. When nicely covered, sauté the pieces in the oil until golden. Remove from the pan and keep warm. Cook the peppers and garlic in the oil remaining in pan until soft and remove with a slotted spoon. Add the red wine and scrape the sides of the pan carefully; add the tomatoes and olives and seasonings. Simmer for 10 minutes, then add the chicken and peppers and cook covered for another half-hour.

TURKEY ROAST

1 6-lb hindquarter roast of turkey
1 cup safflower oil
½ cup chicken broth
¼ cup dry white wine
3 cloves garlic, crushed
3 tbs oregano
Grated rind of 1 lemon

Marinate the turkey in the rest of the ingredients above for four or five hours, turning often. Remove from marinade and bake in a 325° oven for about 2½ to 3 hours, basting frequently with the marinade.

MOCK VEAL SCALLOPINI

(In these days of astronomical food prices, turkey is one of our best protein buys. Economy-wise, the different parts now sold packaged are extremely useful. The breast, for instance, substitutes very nicely for out-of-sight veal in this recipe.)

1	quarter breast of turkey
¼	cup whole wheat flour
¼	tsp paprika
1	tsp Morton's Salt Substitute
2	tbs margarine
2	tbs safflower oil
1½	cups mushrooms, sliced
1	clove garlic, crushed
¾	cup dry white wine
1	tsp lemon juice
¼	tsp Italian herbs
1	tbs parsley, minced

Clear any skin or bone from the turkey and chill for about an hour to make it easier to slice. Cut across the breast to get big flat quarter-inch slices. Dredge with a mixture of the flour, paprika and salt. Brown lightly in a mixture of the margarine and oil; keep browned slices warm while doing the remaining slices. Add mushrooms and garlic to oil remaining in pan after the last slice of meat has been removed; sauté, being careful not to burn the garlic. Return the turkey slices to the pan and add the combined last four ingredients. Simmer over medium heat for about 10 minutes until turkey is tender and juices are somewhat reduced. Serve each slice with some of the juices spooned over.

CURRIED TURKEY BREAST

  1 small turkey breast, about 4 lb
     Salt
 ¼ cup margarine
  2 tbs grated orange rind
 ½ tsp powdered ginger

Season turkey breast with salt and place in glass baking pan. Heat the margarine, orange rind and ginger and pour the mixture over the breast, covering completely. Roast uncovered in a 325° oven for 2 hours, basting as necessary. Cut in bite-sized pieces and add to a sauce mixed from the following:

   1 apple, peeled and chopped
  ¼ cup onion, minced
   1 clove garlic, crushed
  ¼ cup margarine
  ¼ cup whole wheat flour
   1 tsp curry powder, or to taste
 1½ cups chicken broth
  ½ cup milk
     Salt

Sauté the apple, onion and garlic in the margarine till soft. Gradually stir in the flour and curry powder. Add the liquids slowly, and when smooth add the turkey and simmer for 15 minutes. Serve over hot brown rice.

Meat

MARINATED CALF'S LIVER
(Liver is rich in everything from vitamin A to zinc.)

    1 lb calf's liver
  ¾ cup red wine vinegar
    1 tbs onion, chopped
  ½ tsp oregano
    2 cloves garlic, crushed
    1 bay leaf
       Salt to taste
    3 tbs safflower oil
    1 tbs imitation bacon bits

Marinate the liver in everything but the bacon bits and oil. Remove liver from marinade and sauté in the oil over high heat for 2 minutes on each side. Transfer to a heated serving dish and sprinkle with the bacon bits. Add the marinade to the pan and reduce over high heat for 1 minute, then pour over the liver.

BAKED LIVER AND ONIONS

(This adds mineral-rich onions and vitamin-rich parsley, making an exceptionally nutritious dish.)

      2 large Bermuda onions, peeled and sliced
      2 tbs safflower oil
      4 slices calf's liver
        Whole wheat flour, slightly salted
      1 bay leaf
      1 tsp thyme
      6 sprigs parsley
      2 tbs safflower margarine

Arrange the onions in a flat oiled baking dish. Pour the safflower oil over; cover and bake in a 350° oven for about 30 minutes, turning carefully once. Dredge the liver in flour, arrange over the onions and add the herbs and margarine. Cover and bake in a 350° oven for about 20 minutes, uncover and continue baking till the liver is brown.

Parsley Dumplings

      2 cups whole wheat flour
      4 tsps baking powder
     ⅛ tsp each of thyme, nutmeg, sage and cloves
     ¼ cup parsley, chopped fine
      1 tbs margarine
      1 cup boiling water

Mix the dry ingredients, cut in the margarine and mix with enough of the boiling water to make all moist and easy to handle. Drop by teaspoons into the stew.

BEEF LIVER STROGANOFF

(Remember that liver is just about our only source of B_{12}.)

> 1 lb beef liver, membrane removed
> 4 tbs whole wheat flour
> 4 tbs safflower oil
> 1 onion, chopped
> ½ lb mushrooms, sliced
> 2 tbs tomato paste
> ¾ cup beef broth
> 2 tbs sherry
> ½ cup sour cream
>   Salt
> 2 tbs parsley, chopped

Cut the liver into half-inch strips, a half-inch thick. Dredge in flour and keep the flour. Sauté the liver in 3 tbs of the oil till browned on all sides, about 5 minutes. Remove the liver from the pan and add the remaining oil, onion and mushrooms and sauté till soft. Add 1 tbs of the flour and blend in carefully. Add the tomato paste, broth and sherry and cook till mixture thickens; then stir in the sour cream, add the liver and heat through. Salt to taste and serve sprinkled with the chopped parsley.

BEEF STEW WITH PARSLEY DUMPLINGS

> 2 lb stewing beef, cut into 1-inch cubes
>   Whole wheat flour for dredging
> 3 tbs safflower oil
> 1 cup red wine
> 1 cup tomatoes, peeled, seeded and chopped

18 small white onions, peeled
1½ cups carrots, peeled and diced
1 cup green beans, diced
1 large bay leaf
1 tsp thyme
Salt to taste
8 sprigs parsley

Dredge the beef in the flour and brown in the oil, being careful to turn frequently to prevent scorching. Transfer the meat to a pot or casserole. Deglaze the browning pan with the wine, scraping all bits off carefully. Pour over the meat and add enough water to cover. Bring to a boil and simmer gently for 1½ hours. Then add the tomatoes, vegetables, bay leaf and herbs, salt to taste and continue cooking for about 40 minutes or until vegetables are tender. Add the parsley dumplings, cover tightly and let steam over low heat for 10 minutes, turn off the heat and let steam 3 more minutes.

🍂 Vegetarian Dishes

NUTBURGERS

(Whey is a principal source of B_2; the seeds and nuts are rich in minerals.)

    ½ cup sunflower seeds
    ½ cup cashew nuts
    ½ cup walnuts
    ¾ cup almonds
    ½ cup carrot, pureed in blender
    ⅓ cup onion, chopped
    ½ cup celery, minced
    ¼ cup whey
    1 egg
    1 clove garlic, crushed
    ½ tsp sage
    ½ tsp chili powder
       Large pinch each of cumin and curry powder
    ½ tbs parsley, minced
    1 tbs safflower oil

Combine the seeds, nuts, carrot, onion and celery. Put through a grinder or blender with the whey and eggs. Add

the seasonings and parsley, shape into patties and sauté
in the oil.

EGGPLANT CASSEROLE
(B₁ and manganese in those walnuts, C in the tomatoes)

1¼ lb eggplant
2 cloves garlic, crushed
¼ cup safflower oil
1 red onion, peeled and thinly sliced
1½ cups plum tomatoes, peeled (save all juice) and thinly sliced
¼ cup dry white wine
Salt
¾ cup walnut pieces
¼ lb fontina cheese, cut in strips
⅛ lb mozzarella cheese, cut in strips

Trim the stems from the eggplant and slice lengthwise, a
half-inch thick. Salt on both sides and let stand for a
half-hour, then drain, pressing out the excess moisture.
Mix the garlic with the oil and brush both sides of the
eggplant slices with it. Sauté the eggplant in the remaining oil for several minutes on each side and remove from
pan. Add the onion and cook over high heat till transparent; then add the tomatoes with their juices and the
wine. Cook for several minutes over high heat; then salt
to taste. Pour this sauce into a shallow casserole and
arrange the eggplant slices evenly over it, making one
overlapping layer. Spread the walnuts over this, then the
strips of fontina and finally the mozzarella. Bake for 30
minutes in a 350° oven.

VEGETABLE BURGERS
(B vitamins in the wheat germ, zinc in the mushrooms, more B in the cheese)

    ¾ cup wheat germ
    ¾ cup grated Monterey Jack cheese
    3 medium-sized zucchini, grated
    2 eggs, lightly beaten
    ⅓ cup mushrooms, chopped
    3 tbs onion, chopped
    ¼ tsp each thyme and rosemary, crushed
       Salt to taste
    1 tbs safflower oil

Combine all ingredients except oil, mixing well. Form into four patties and sauté in the oil till brown and well heated, about 4 minutes on each side. These can be served in whole wheat buns or simply topped with yoghurt and perhaps mustard.

MUSHROOMS ON TOAST
(zinc-rich mushrooms, vitamin- and mineral-rich parsley)

  1½ lb fresh, firm mushrooms
    4 tbs safflower oil
    4 tbs parsley, minced
    2 cloves garlic, crushed
       Salt
  2½ tbs safflower margarine
    2 tbs fresh lemon juice
  1½ tbs wine vinegar

2 tbs cilantro (fresh coriander leaves, sometimes
    called Chinese parsley), chopped
4 slices whole wheat toast

Stem and halve the washed mushrooms. In a bowl mix
them with the oil, parsley, garlic and salt to taste. Melt
the margarine in a skillet and sauté the mushrooms
briskly for 5 minutes, stirring. Add the lemon juice, vinegar and cilantro and cook another 5 minutes. Serve on
the toast with any remaining liquid poured over.

VEGETABLE CURRY KINARIWALA

  1 large onion, finely chopped
  2 cloves garlic, crushed
    1-inch piece of fresh ginger, grated
½ green pepper, chopped
  1 tsp fresh basil leaves, chopped (or ½ tsp dried)
¼ green chili pepper, chopped
  3 tbs safflower oil
½ tsp turmeric
  2 small potatoes, cubed
½ small cauliflower, chopped
    Salt
  1 cup peas
  2 tbs coriander (Chinese parsley), chopped (or 1 tbs
    dried)

Sauté the first six ingredients above in the oil till golden,
then add turmeric and sauté a few more minutes. Add
the next three ingredients. Sauté a few minutes on high
heat, add water to just cover, and salt to taste. Lower heat
and simmer. After 5 minutes add peas, cook till tender,
then add coriander. Serve with brown rice.

BURRITOS
(Wheat germ provides plentiful B vitamins.)

½ cup onion, finely chopped
3 small zucchini, chopped
1 4-oz can green chilies, chopped
½ tsp oregano leaves, crushed
1 tsp basil, finely chopped (or ½ tsp dried)
¼ tsp cumin seed, ground
2 tbs safflower oil
1 cup Monterey Jack cheese, grated
¾ cup wheat germ
Salt to taste
6 large flour tortillas
Yoghurt
Parsley, minced

Sauté the vegetables and seasonings in 1 tablespoon of the oil for about 5 minutes. Add the cheese and the wheat germ, stirring till cheese melts. Salt to taste. Divide the mixture onto the tortillas, then fold tortillas over to enclose the filling completely. Heat the other tablespoon of oil and sauté the burritos, adding oil if needed. When golden brown, serve topped with a generous dollop of yoghurt and sprinkled with parsley.

MUSHROOMS POLONAISE
(one more zinc-rich mushroom dish)

½ cup safflower margarine
1 lb mushrooms, sliced
1 medium onion, minced

3 tbs whole wheat flour
1 cup yoghurt
¼ tsp nutmeg
¼ cup bread crumbs (whole wheat) stirred in some melted margarine
3 tbs parsley, minced

Melt margarine, add mushrooms and brown. Add onion, cook a little more, then work in the flour and cook a few minutes more. Add the yoghurt carefully over low heat, stirring till thickened. Add nutmeg and pour into flat casserole, sprinkle with bread crumbs and parsley and bake 35 minutes at 350°.

ONION TART

2 cups Spanish onions, chopped
1 tbs safflower margarine
1 tbs safflower oil
¼ tsp Morton's Salt Substitute
1 cup Gruyère cheese, shredded
Baked 7-inch pastry shell
½ tbs anchovies, chopped
1 tbs ripe olives, sliced
1 tbs Parmesan cheese, grated
1 tbs parsley, chopped

Sauté the onions in the margarine and oil until just tender—do not brown. Salt to taste. Spread half the Gruyère in the bottom of the pastry shell, top with half the onions and repeat. Scatter the anchovies and olives over, and sprinkle with the Parmesan. Bake in a 350° oven for 20 minutes and serve sprinkled with the parsley.

Eggs

OMELETTE FINES HERBES
(*As mentioned earlier, eggs are the food richest in all nutrients.*)

    2 eggs
    1 tbs parsley, minced
    ½ tbs fresh rosemary, minced
    ½ tbs chives, minced
    1 tbs safflower oil
       Morton's Salt Substitute or Vegesalt

Eggs require a light touch; a perfect omelette doesn't just happen. This recipe is for one, as a small omelette is easiest to handle. Beat the eggs in a bowl with a wire whisk, add the herbs. Put the oil in a heavy omelette pan, 8 or 9 inches in diameter. A cast iron pan covered with enamel is best. Heat the oil in the pan, rolling and tilting so the oil covers the bottom. When quite hot add the eggs and cook over medium heat. Lift the edges with a spatula to let the eggs flow to the bottom while tilting the pan, and shake it occasionally to keep them from sticking. Be very careful not to overcook; eggs need just the smallest amount of cooking. When the top is just barely set but still moist-looking, fold the omelette over, let it rest in the pan for a minute or so, and slide it onto a hot plate.

MUSHROOM OMELETS
(a combination rich in zinc as well as the other minerals)

    2 tbs onion, minced
    3 tbs margarine
    8 large fresh mushrooms, sliced
       Pinch of thyme
    ½ tsp dill weed
       Salt to taste
    1 cup yoghurt
    8 eggs
    ¼ cup milk
    3 tbs safflower oil
       Parsley, chopped

Sauté the onion in the margarine till golden, add the mushrooms and simmer until the mushrooms are tender. Add the thyme and dill and salt to taste, and gradually stir in the yoghurt. Keep warm while beating the eggs with the milk to make 4 individual omelets in the safflower oil; divide the mushroom filling between them and fold over. Garnish with the chopped parsley and serve.

PIPERADE

  1 onion, finely chopped
  2 cloves garlic, crushed
  4 tomatoes, peeled, seeded and sliced thin
  1 green pepper, chopped fine
  1 chili pepper, chopped
     Salt
  6 eggs
  1 tbs safflower margarine

Sauté the onion in a heavy skillet until transparent; add the garlic, tomatoes, peppers and salt to taste. Simmer for about an hour or until the liquid from the tomatoes has disappeared. Beat the eggs with a wire whisk and scramble them lightly in the margarine. Combine the two mixtures and serve with whole wheat toast.

OMELETTE PROVENÇALE

  1 onion, chopped
  2 cloves garlic, crushed
  2 tbs safflower oil
  1 tbs olive oil
  2 bay leaves, crumbled
  8 medium tomatoes, peeled, seeded and chopped
  ½ tsp basil
  ½ tsp tarragon
  2 tbs parsley, minced

5 black olives, sliced
8 eggs
  Safflower oil for cooking omelets
  Salt to taste

Sauté the onion and garlic in the safflower and olive oil, add the bay leaves and cook a few minutes more. Add the tomatoes, basil, tarragon, parsley and olives and cook for about 45 minutes, stirring occasionally. Keep hot while making 4 individual omelets in remaining oil. Spoon the tomato mixture over the barely set eggs and fold the omelets over.

CORN SOUFFLÉ

2 large fresh ears of corn
2 tbs margarine
3 tbs cornstarch
1 cup milk
  Salt to taste
4 eggs, separated

Scrape the corn off the cobs with a sharp knife, then remove all the pulp and juice with the back of the knife. Make a roux of the margarine and cornstarch, remove from heat and gradually add the milk. Salt to taste and cook, stirring constantly, till thickened. Remove from heat and beat in the egg yolks one at a time. Add the corn, fold in the stiffly beaten egg whites and turn into an oiled, flour-dusted 2-quart soufflé dish. Bake in a 375° oven for 30 minutes.

EGGS FLORENTINE
(vitamin A and C as well as all the nutrients of the eggs)

>   3 tbs safflower oil
>   2 lb fresh spinach, well washed
>   Melted margarine
>   4 eggs
>   4 tbs Parmesan cheese, grated
>   1 tbs margarine
>   1 tbs whole wheat flour
>   1 cup milk
>   Pinch thyme
>   Small piece bay leaf, crumbled
>   Salt

Heat the oil in a large pan, add the spinach leaves and cover tightly. Cook over low heat for 5 minutes, then stir to coat all the leaves with oil. Cook a few more minutes until wilted. Put the spinach in a shallow glass baking dish and with the back of a spoon make four hollows. Pour a little melted margarine in the hollows and break an egg into each. Sprinkle the cheese over them. Make a roux of the margarine and flour, add the milk and seasonings and stir till thickened. Pour sauce over the eggs and bake in oven for 10 minutes. Serve at once.

EGGS AU GRATIN

>   3 tbs safflower margarine
>   3 tbs whole wheat flour
> 1½ cups milk, heated

1½ cups grated cheddar cheese
 8 eggs
 ½ cup bread crumbs mixed with 2 tbs melted margarine

Make a roux of the margarine and flour, cook a few minutes and gradually stir in the hot milk. Pour half the sauce into an oiled baking dish, sprinkle with half the cheese. Break the eggs over the sauce, and cover with the remaining sauce and cheese. Top with the bread crumbs and bake for about 12 minutes in a 350° oven.

CHEESE SOUFFLÉ

  3 tbs safflower margarine
  4 tbs whole wheat flour
1¼ cups hot milk
  1 tsp salt substitute
     Dash cayenne
  ½ cup grated sharp cheddar
  2 egg yolks, beaten well
  2 egg whites, beaten till they hold a peak

Make a roux of the margarine and flour, cook a minute or two and gradually add the milk to make a smooth sauce. Salt to taste and add the cayenne and cheese, stirring till perfectly smooth. Remove from heat and cool slightly before adding the egg yolks slowly. Fold in the egg whites and pour into an oiled soufflé dish. Bake in a 325° oven for one hour.

ONION AND HERB FRITTATA

    1 red onion, chopped coarsely
    2 tbs safflower oil
    ½ cup parsley, chopped
    ⅓ cup chives, snipped
    ¼ tsp dried basil (2 tsp fresh if available)
    4 eggs
       Salt to taste

Sauté the onion in the oil and add the parsley, chives and basil. Sauté, stirring, a few minutes, and arrange evenly in the pan. Beat the eggs with a whisk and pour carefully over the herbs. Turn the heat as low as possible, cover the pan and cook 10 to 15 minutes or until eggs are set. Flip the pan over, holding the lid firmly, so that the frittata falls into the lid. Slide it back into the pan to brown the other side and turn out onto a heated serving plate. Salt to taste. Just before serving, preferably at room temperature, cut it into wedges.

 **Vegetables**

SCALLOPED POTATOES
(B vitamins in the wheat germ and cheese; potassium in the potatoes)

> 1 cup rich milk
> 1 small onion, finely chopped
> 2 tbs chives, snipped
> ½ cup Swiss cheese, grated
> 4 potatoes, peeled and sliced thin (retain the peels for a vitamin-packed broth)
>   Salt to taste
>   Wheat germ
> 1 rounded tbs safflower margarine

Mix the milk, onion, chives and cheese. Oil a casserole and place a layer of potatoes on the bottom. Salt them and pour over some of the milk mixture; repeat layers, ending with the milk mixture on top. Sprinkle generously with wheat germ and dot with the margarine. Cover and bake for 1 hour at 350°; uncover and bake 1 hour more.

SPINACH TIMBALES

    1 tbs margarine
    2 tbs whole wheat flour
    2 cups scalded milk
2½ cups cooked chopped spinach
    4 eggs, well beaten
    1 tbs onion, chopped fine
       Salt to taste

Make a roux of the margarine and flour, cook a few minutes, then add the milk to make a smooth sauce. Add the rest of the ingredients and pour into oiled custard cups set in a pan of hot water. Bake for 40 minutes at 375°.

VEGETABLES WITH GREEK MARINADE
(*This is another way to prepare any number of vegetables, such as carrots, zucchini, green beans and leeks. Sliced fresh mushrooms add well to any one of them— or to any combination of them. The vegetables should be cut into lengthwise strips and attractively arranged on a serving dish.*)

    2 cups white wine
  ⅓ cup olive oil
  ⅓ cup safflower oil
    1 tsp Morton's Salt Substitute or Vegesalt
    1 bay leaf
    6 or 7 peppercorns
    1 tsp thyme
  ¼ tsp tarragon
    3 cloves garlic, crushed

2 tbs lemon juice
Parsley, minced (optional)

Combine all the ingredients except the parsley and pour over the vegetables in a skillet. Add just enough water to cover, and simmer till the vegetables are barely cooked —tender but still a little crisp. Drain and chill and perhaps garnish with some minced parsley.

LIMA BEANS
(Lima beans are valuable for their B_6, C, potassium and molybdenum.)

1 lb dried lima beans
   Water to cover beans
½ cup onion, chopped
1 tsp celery leaves, minced
1 tbs parsley, minced
1 bay leaf, crumbled
¼ tsp thyme
   Pinch marjoram
   Salt to taste
½ qt cold water

Soak the beans overnight in water to cover amply. Drain and put the beans, along with all the rest of the ingredients, in a heavy pot. Bring to a boil, then simmer for at least 1½ hours or until the beans are done. Remove from heat, let cool somewhat, then cover and let stand at room temperature for several hours, until liquid is absorbed and beans tender. When ready to serve reheat.

RED CABBAGE
(Cabbage gives us B_6, C, inositol, sulfur and selenium.)

> 1   lb red cabbage, shredded
> 1   small onion, chopped
> 2   small green apples, peeled, cored and chopped coarsely
> ¼   cup safflower margarine
> 2   tbs brown sugar
> 2   tbs cider vinegar
>   Pinch each of ground cloves, cinnamon and nutmeg
>   Salt to taste
> ⅓   cup beer

Sauté the cabbage, onion and apples in the margarine for about 10 minutes. Add the rest of the ingredients, mixing well, and simmer covered for 1 hour. An occasional stir may be necessary. This is even better when it is allowed to stand awhile and is then reheated.

CABBAGE FRICASSEE

> 1   large cabbage, outer leaves removed, cored and grated
> 1   tbs safflower oil
> 1   tbs safflower margarine
> 1   tbs lemon juice
> 1½ tbs margarine mixed with 1½ tbs lemon juice

Simmer the cabbage, covered, with the oil, margarine and lemon juice. It should be just tender in about 10 minutes. Then stir in the additional margarine and lemon juice.

BAKED SWEET POTATOES
(Sweet potatoes contain B_6 and E.)

    2 good-sized sweet potatoes
    3 tbs safflower margarine
  ⅓ cup rich milk
  ½ cup minced smoked ham
      Salt to taste

Bake the potatoes in a 400° oven for 40 minutes, or till tender. Cut them in half lengthwise and remove the pulp, being careful to preserve the shells. Mash the potato with the margarine and milk, add the ham and salt to taste and stuff the shells. Bake at 425° for 15 minutes.

VEGETABLE SOUFFLÉ
(This simple recipe can be used as a way of preparing any number of different vegetables—singly or in combinations.)

  ¼ cup whole wheat flour
  ¼ tsp Morton's Salt Substitute or Vegesalt
  ½ cup Perfect Mayonnaise (see page 133)
  ¼ cup milk
    1 cup finely chopped vegetables (broccoli, green pepper, green beans, spinach, for example)
    4 egg whites

Stir the flour and salt into the mayonnaise gently—don't overmix. Add the milk and vegetables. Beat the egg whites till they hold a peak, and fold into the mayonnaise mixture. Pour into an oiled soufflé dish and bake for 40 minutes at 325°.

SPINACH WITH CHEESE
(*Spinach gives us vitamins A, C and E, magnesium and potassium.*)

    2 lb spinach, washed, leaves only
    1 onion, minced
    6 tbs margarine
    1 cup mozzarella cheese, cut in thin strips
    1 cup Parmesan cheese, grated
       Salt to taste
    1 hard-boiled egg, grated

Cook the spinach in a very little boiling water for about one minute, then drain well to remove all the excess moisture. Chop coarsely. Sauté the onion in the margarine, add the spinach and salt and cook for several minutes. Take the pan off the heat and add the cheeses, stirring vigorously till they are melted. Top with the hard-boiled egg.

GREENS SOUTHERN STYLE
(*These greens are rich in vitamins A and C, also provide E and calcium.*)

    1 bunch mustard greens
    1 bunch turnip greens
    1 bunch beet tops
    1 bunch parsley
    1 bunch watercress
    1 tbs safflower oil
    1 tbs whole wheat flour

1 onion, chopped
½ cup lean baked ham, diced fine

Place the washed greens in a colander and rinse with cold water. Shake the excess water off and put the greens in a heavy pan with about ⅓ cup of water. Cover the pan tightly and cook for about 15 minutes over medium heat. Drain in a colander and save the liquid. Chop the greens. Make a roux of the oil and flour, browning well. Add the onion and continue cooking, stirring constantly, for 5 minutes. Gradually add 1 cup of the reserved liquid, then stir in the ham and greens.

🍂 Breads and Such

WHOLE WHEAT BREAD

    2 pkgs active dry yeast
    ¼ cup lukewarm water
    1½ tsp salt
    2 tbs safflower oil
    2 cups lukewarm to hot water
    1 cup unbleached flour
    4½ cups 100% stone-ground whole wheat flour

Dissolve yeast in the ¼ cup of water, add salt, oil and rest of water. Add the white flour, blend well. Then add the rest of the flour little by little. If dough is still sticky when all the flour has been added, sprinkle in a little more whole wheat flour. (Bread seems to be temperamental, perhaps by reason of the weather, and the amount of flour necessary seems to vary.) Turn onto a floured board and knead until dough is elastic, or, if available, use a Cuisinart and divide the dough into two parts, kneading half and then combining part of the kneaded dough with the other half so that the dough is evenly

exercised. Place in an oiled bowl, cover with a cloth and
let rise in a protected place (perhaps in your cool oven)
until doubled in bulk, about 1½ hours. Repeat the kneading, divide dough in half and place in two oiled loaf pans.
Let rise again until nearly double, about ¾ of an hour.
Bake at 400° for 45 minutes or until the loaf sounds hol-
low when rapped and is golden brown. Remove immediately from pans and cool on wire racks.

OATMEAL BREAD
(Oatmeal provides B₁ and E as well as zinc.)

    2 pkgs active dry yeast
½ cup lukewarm water
    2 tsps salt
    1 tbs safflower oil
    1 cup Old Fashioned Quaker Oats
    2 cups boiling water
½ cup blackstrap molasses
    3 cups unbleached flour
    3 cups 100% stone-ground whole wheat flour

Dissolve the yeast in the half-cup of lukewarm water.
Mix the salt, oil and oats and pour over, stirring, the
boiling water. Let this mixture stand for an hour, then
add the dissolved yeast, the molasses and all the flour.
Beat hard, or divide and put in Cuisinart. Place in an
oiled bowl and let rise in a protected place until doubled
in size. Repeat the beating, then put dough in two loaf
pans to let it rise again till double in bulk. Bake in a 350°
oven for 1 hour. Cool on wire rack.

CORN BREAD
(Cornmeal contains vitamin B_1.)

   1 egg, separated
  ½ cup yellow cornmeal
1¼ cups skim milk
  ¾ cup whole wheat flour
  ¼ cup soy flour (low fat soy powder)
  1 tbs baking powder
  ½ tsp Morton's Salt Substitute

Beat the egg white till it peaks. Mix the other ingredients with the egg yolk, beating well. When smooth, fold into the egg white and pour into an 8-inch oiled glass baking pan. Bake in a 425° oven for 20 minutes. Serve immediately, cut into squares or wedges.

DARK RUSSIAN RYE BREAD

  2 pkgs active dry yeast
  ½ cup lukewarm water
  2 cups lukewarm water
  ½ cup skim milk powder
  ¼ cup blackstrap molasses
  4 cups rye flour
  2 cups raisins, soaked for 10 minutes and drained
  ¼ cup margarine
     Rind of 2 oranges, grated
1½ tbs anise, crushed
  2 tsp Morton's Salt Substitute
  3 cups unbleached flour
     Very strong coffee

Dissolve the yeast in the half-cup of water. In a large bowl mix the 2 cups of water, the dry milk and the molasses and add the dissolved yeast. Add 2 cups of the rye flour and the raisins, then the margarine, orange rind, anise and salt. Beat in the remaining rye flour and the unbleached 3 cups. Turn onto a floured board and knead for 5 minutes. Turn the bowl over the dough and wait 15 minutes, then knead another 10 minutes. Let it rise in an oiled bowl, covered with a towel, for an hour. Knead again and divide into three round loaves. Place on a baking sheet that's been dusted with cornmeal, slash the tops of each loaf with a sharp knife in a cross, cover with damp towels and let rise again for an hour. Brush the loaves with very strong coffee and bake for 50 minutes at 375°. Cool on wire racks.

 **Sweets**

CARROT CAKE
(Vitamin A in the carrots; see above for walnuts!)

    1 cup softened safflower margarine
    1 cup honey
 1½ cups carrots, grated fine
  ⅔ cup walnuts, toasted and chopped
    1 tsp ground cinnamon
  ½ tsp nutmeg
 2½ cups unbleached flour, sifted
    3 tsps baking powder
  ½ tsp salt
  ⅓ cup warm water
    4 egg whites, lightly beaten

Beat the margarine and honey until light and fluffy, then stir in the carrots and nuts. Sift together the other dry ingredients and add to the mixture alternately with the water, folding in the flour rather than beating it in. Add the lightly beaten egg whites and turn all into an oiled and floured 11×15–inch pan. Bake for 35 minutes in a 350° oven. Cool on a wire rack.

POACHED PEARS
(vitamin C)

4 Anjou pears, unpeeled
Water to cover
½ cup honey
1 tsp cinnamon
¼ tsp ginger
1 box fresh raspberries, washed
2 tbs Marsala wine

Place the pears in a saucepan, cover with water and add the honey, cinnamon and ginger. Poach for a half-hour or till a fork easily pierces the pears. Run the berries and Marsala through a blender, place the chilled pears in individual bowls and pour the sauce over them.

WALNUT TARTS
(Walnuts provide zinc, manganese and magnesium.)

½ cup walnuts
2 eggs, separated
¼ cup hcney
Pinch of salt
¼ cup whole wheat bread crumbs

Grind the walnuts. Beat the egg yolks and add to the honey. Beat the egg whites till they form peaks and fold them, with the walnuts and bread crumbs, into the egg-yolk–honey mixture. Spoon into an oiled pan in four tarts and bake in a preheated 325° oven for 45 minutes.

SAUTÉED BANANAS
(*potassium*)

> 3 tbs safflower margarine
> 2 tbs dark Myers's rum
> 2 tbs honey
> 4 bananas, halved lengthwise

Melt the margarine, add the rum and honey and mix in a skillet. Lay the cut bananas in the mixture and sauté gently, turning once. Lift out carefully when browned. Serve on dessert plates.

OATMEAL SESAME COOKIES

> 1½ cups oatmeal
> 1½ cups whole wheat flour
> ¼ cup sesame seeds
> 1½ tsp baking powder
> 1½ tsp cinnamon
> ¼ tsp salt
> 2 apples, cored and chopped
> ½ cup honey
> ½ cup safflower oil
> 1 egg, beaten
> ⅓ cup milk

In a large bowl mix the oatmeal, flour, sesame seeds, baking powder, cinnamon and salt. Stir in the apples. Mix the honey, oil, egg and milk, and stir into the mixture. Drop by the rounded teaspoonful onto an ungreased cookie sheet and bake for 12 minutes at 375°. Cool on a wire rack.

Index

[*A recipe index follows the general index.*]

Academy of Orthomolecular
    Psychiatry, 10
Acetaldehyde insult, 90–91
Acetylcholine, 32
Acidophilus, 69
Acids, 76, 100
Additives, 37, 49, 53, 76, 101
Adrenal gland, 42, 65
Adrenaline, 82, 97
Affluence, 59–60
Aging, 93–98, 106–107
Alcohol, 82, 86–92, 97
Alcohol tolerance, 35
Alcoholics Anonymous (AA) 86,
    87, 90–92
Alcoholism, 37, 41, 85–92
Allergies, 37, 41, 47, 90, 100
Aluminum, 37, 70, 104, 117
Amenorrhea, 105
American diet, 54–56, 76
American Health Foundation, 58
American Heart Association, 57
American Medical Association
    (AMA), 37, 43, 85
American way of life, 79–80
Amino acids, 19, 61–62, 84
Anemia, 35, 60
Angina, 38
Animal fat, 53
Animal foods, 56
Animal liver, 65, 68, 83

Animal products, 60
Animal protein, 54, 61, 63
Ankle swelling, 39
Antabuse, 88
Antianxiety agents, 83, 89
Antibiotics, 50
Antimicrobial preservatives, 49
Antioxidants, 31, 49, 95
Antitoxins, 43, 69
Anxiety, 35, 83, 89
Appetite, 18
Apricots, 65
Arteries, 37, 96, 97
Arteriosclerosis, 96
Arthritic's Cookbook, The, 11,
    93
Arthritis, 28, 31, 36, 99–102
Artichokes, 57
Artificial flavoring, 51–52
Asbestos, 37
Ascorbic acid, *see* Vitamin C
Asparagus, 57
Aspirin, 38, 82, 99
Atherosclerosis, 96
Atkins diet, 72–73

Bacon, 50
Bacterial infection, 100
Balanced diet, 17, 68
Bananas, 65, 68

Banks, Jane, 11, 93, 117
Barbiturates, 88, 89
Barley, 83
Beans, 57, 60–62, 54, 68–69
Beef heart, 83
Beef liver, 68, 83
Beer, 97
Behavior, 40–41, 86, 97
BHA, 49
BHT, 49
Biochemical analysis, 34–35
Biochemical diagnosis, 89–90
Biochemical individuality, 16
Biochemical treatment, 15, 16
Biochemistry, 10, 35, 60
Biotin, 62
Birth-control pill, 44
Bismuth, 24
Blindness, 42
Blood cells, 31
Blood clots, 44
Blood glucose levels, 42, 43
Blood histamine levels, 89
Blood pressure, 37–40, 44, 48,
    96, 106
Blood sugar (glucose), 22, 35, 41–
    43, 65–66, 86
    tolerance factor, 29, 79, 89–90,
    106
Body chemistry, 34
Body fat, 75
Body weight, 72–80
Bone development, 46–47
Bone growth, 106
Bouillon, 77
Brain, 10, 40, 42, 52, 87
Brain Bio Center, 15–17, 34, 103
Brain Bio Center studies
    of alcoholism, 90–91
    of blood pressure, 40
    of dream recall, 84

of inositol, 83
of mental illness, 36, 37
of vitamin B, 84
of pyroluria, 41
Bran, 59, 64
Bread, 75
Breakfast, 52–53, 59
Breast cancer, 53, 58
Brewer's yeast, 29, 36, 64, 68, 79,
    96, 101
    dosage for adults, 106
    pollution and, 69
    as source of selenium, 65
Broccoli, 57, 61, 65, 77
Brown rice, 61
Brussels sprouts, 57, 65, 95
BVO (brominated vegetable oil),
    50

Cabbage, 69, 76, 83, 101
Cadmium, 18, 22–24, 29, 37, 43,
    48
Calciferol, 27
    See also Vitamin D
Calcium, 18, 20, 42, 43, 46–48,
    96
    sources of, 20–21, 62, 70, 114
Calcium dolomite, 21, 32, 106
Calories, 46, 53, 56, 73–76
Cameron, Ewan, 30
Cancer, 29, 30, 37, 53, 58
    copper and, 41
    food coloring and, 51
    preservatives and, 49–50, 82
Canned foods, 47, 59, 68
Cantaloupe, 65
Carbohydrates, 56, 61, 66, 90
Carbon monoxide, 43
Cardamom, 64
Cardiovascular disease, *see*
    Heart disease

Carotene, *see* Vitamin A
Carrots, 57, 70–71, 76, 77, 96
Cauliflower, 57
Celery, 70–71, 76
Cereals, 52–53
Cerebral allergies, 41, 90
Cheese, 77
Chelating agent, 48
Chemicals, 47–53
Chest pain, 39
Chick peas, 69
Chicken, 100
Children, 105
Chinese food, 52, 64
Chloral, 89
Chlorine, 71
Cholesterol, 28, 30, 39, 53, 57–
    60, 63, 94, 96, 97
Choline, 27, 32, 43, 62, 66
Chrome, 24
Chromium, 17, 22, 43, 63, 66,
    95, 96
    sources of, 22, 29, 36, 48, 106,
    115
Cider Vinegar diet, 73
Cigarettes, 44
Cirrhosis of the liver, 86
Citrus fruits, 64, 95
Clayton Foundation, 63, 99
Cloves, 64
Cobalt, 17–18, 22
Coffee, 84
Colds, 29, 30
Collagen, 29
Colon, cancer of, 53, 58
Consumer Protection Agency, 49
Convulsions, 35
Cooking, 17, 37, 70, 117
Copper, 17, 24, 35, 41, 44, 89
    arthritis and, 31, 100
    in cooking utensils, 70, 117

in drinking water, 71, 104
hypertension and, 39
in plumbing, 37, 96
schizophrenia and, 10, 41
sulfur and, 101
vitamin C and, 29, 41
in vitamin supplements, 104
zinc and, 19, 24, 41, 38, 100
Copper serum, 41, 100
Copper toxicity, 35
Corn germ, 64

Dairy products, 65, 100
Dalmane, 89
Dates, 64
Davis, Adelle, 54
Davis, Donald, 53
DDT, 69
Deaner, 32
Deanol, 95
Dehydration, 87
Dental requirements, 47
Dentine, 29
Depressants, 88
Depression, 35, 38, 41, 91
DES, 50
Desserts, 77
Diabetes, 29, 37, 42, 71
Diet, 16, 39, 54–63, 72–78
    aging and, 93–94
    alcoholism and, 91
    for arthritis, 100–102
    balanced, 17, 68
    health and, 103
    for heart disease, 64–65
    hypoglycemia and, 35, 43, 65–
    67, 75–76
    inadequate, 45, 53, 54
    junk food, 54, 63, 75, 103
    low in salt, 106
    meatless, 60

Diet *(cont.)*
  salt-free, 64
  sugar and, 65–66, 75
  vegetarian, 59–62, 74
Diet for a Small Planet, 60, 62
Dietary cholesterol, 53
Dinner, 77
Dipstick, 36
Diseases, 35, 69, 101
  infectious, 41, 100
Distilled water, 71
Diuretics, 39
Doctors, 16, 34–38, 47
Dolomite, 21, 32, 106
Dong, Collin, 93, 94, 100
Doriden, 89
Dream recall, 35, 41, 84, 105
Drinking, alcoholic, 85–92
Drinking Man's Diet, 73
Drinking water, 37, 38, 70–71, 76, 104
Drugs, 38, 43, 69, 87–89, 91, 99
  sedatives, 82, 83

Eating habits, 54–55, 80
EDTA, 48
Eggs, 62–65, 75, 101
Eggshells, 64, 70
Elements, 96, 101
El-Meligi, Dr., 36
Emotions, 35, 40–41, 68
Emulsifiers, 50–51
Endocrine glands, 42
Energy, 56
Environment, 43
Enzymes, 18, 88
Epilepsy, 35, 41, 89
Ethyl alcohol, 91
Exercise, 40, 43, 63, 66, 78, 82
  for aging, 94, 96–97

Experiential World Inventory test, 36, 90

Fats, 53, 57–58, 61, 63, 64, 97, 101
Fava beans, 69
Fiber, 59
Fingernails, white spots on, 35, 61, 105
Fish, 100
Fish liver, 65
Fish liver oil, 31, 96
Flagyl, 87–88
Flour, 48
Fluorescent lighting, 37
Folic acid, 27, 29, 32, 60, 62, 106
  food processing and, 47
Food additives, 37, 49, 53, 76, 101
Food allergies, 41, 47
Food colorings, 51
Food and Drug Administration, 48–49, 51, 53
Food industry, 52–54, 59, 80
Food pollution, 37, 43
Food processing, 17, 47–53
Foods
  canned, 47, 59, 68
  frozen, 47–48, 59
  loss of nutrients in, 47–48
  natural, 56, 63–64
  purchase of, 68–70, 75
  selection of, 54, 103
  strong-smelling, 65
  vitamins and minerals in, 108–115
Frozen foods, 47–48, 59
Fruit juice, 64, 77
Fruits, 56, 59, 64, 65, 68, 77
  arthritis and, 100

citrus, 64, 95
  sugar in, 97
Functional hypoglycemia, 41–43, 65–67
  See also Hypoglycemia

Garlic, 65
Gas stoves, 37
Georgetown University, 18
Geriatrics, 95, 106
Ginger, 64
Glucose, 22, 35, 41–43, 65–66, 86
Glucose tolerance factor, 29, 79, 89–90, 106
Goiters, 69
Gori, Gio B., 58
Grains, 56, 59–61, 64, 100
Grapefruit, 83
GRAS (Generally Recognized as Safe), 49
Green peas, 69, 83
Green peppers, 65, 76, 95, 101
Green salad, 77

Hair loss, 35
Hallucinations, 41
Ham, 50
Hard water, 71
Hardening of the arteries, 37, 96, 97
Harris, Seale, 66
Headaches, 35, 38, 44, 52
Health, 97, 103
Health faddists, 53
Health food stores, 48
Health menaces, 37–44, 85
Heart attacks, 24, 38–39, 63–65
Heart disease, 37–40, 53, 63–65, 71, 96

Heavy elements, 101
Heavy metals, 22, 24, 100
Herbs, 70, 77
Herring, 65
High blood pressure, 37–40, 44, 48, 96, 106
Histamine, 35, 40–41, 89, 90
Hoffer-Osmond Diagnostic Test, 90
Honey, 75
Hops, 90
Hormones, 50, 99, 105
Hot dogs, 50, 52, 64
Hydrocortisone, 99
Hydrogenized products, 63
Hyperactivity, 15, 18, 22, 37, 41
Hypertension, 37, 39–40, 63–65, 96
Hypochondriasis, 90
Hypoglycemia, 35, 38, 41–43, 65–67, 75–76
  alcohol and, 86, 87, 90, 91
  chromium and, 22, 66
  sugar and, 37, 65–66

Ice cream, 52, 73
Infants, 104
Infection, bacterial, 100
Infectious diseases, 41
Inositol, 27, 32, 39, 83, 106
  sources of, 83, 112
Insomnia, 35, 38, 81–83, 97
Insulin, 22, 42, 66
Iodine, 17–18, 43, 69
Iodized salt, 105
IQ, 97
Iron, 17, 19, 31, 61, 106
  sources of, 19, 48, 71, 112–113
Irrational behavior, 35
Irritability, 41
Isbell, Harris, 89

Japanese food, 52, 64
Joint pain, 35, 52
Joints, 31
Juices, 64, 70–71, 77
Junk food, 54, 63, 75, 103

Kale, 69, 73, 105
Kelp, 69
Kidneys (human), 69, 86
Kitchen knives, 70
Kunin, Richard A., 11

Lacto-ovo-vegetarian, 60
Lacto-vegetarian, 60
Lappe, Frances Moore, 60
Lead, 18, 22–23, 29, 43, 100, 117
Lead poisoning, 22–23, 43
Learning ability, 97
Learning disabilities, 15
Lecithin, 48, 69, 73, 96, 106
Leg cramps, 32
Legumes, 68–69
Lemon juice, 77
Lentils, 64, 68–69
Lettuce, 71, 76
Librium, 83, 89
Lima beans, 57, 68–69
Linus Pauling Institute of
    Science and Medicine, 30
Liquor, *see* Alcohol
Liver
    animal, 65, 68, 83
    fish, 65, 31, 96
Liver (human), 43, 61, 69, 86
Liver, cirrhosis of, 86
Longevity, 94, 98
Lotusate, 89
Lucretius, 47
Lunch, 75–76

Luncheon meats, 50
Lung cancer, 37

Macrobiotic diet, 73
Madison Avenue, 46, 68
Magnesium, 18, 21, 39, 43, 64,
    106
    cholesterol and, 58, 63
    glucose metabolism and, 42
    sources of, 64, 70, 71, 114
Malnutrition, 54
Malt, 90
Manganese, 10, 17, 35, 43, 66
    aging and, 94, 95
    arthritis and, 100, 105
    blood pressure and, 106
    copper and, 41
    sources of, 20, 38, 48, 64, 113
    for teenagers, 105
    zinc and, 38, 41
Manic-depressives, 41
Mann, George, 72
Maraschino cherries, 51
Mass media, 54
Mayo Diet, 73
Mayonnaise, 70
Meat, 46, 49–50, 57, 59, 61, 77
    lack of, 60–61, 105
Meatless diet, 60, 100
Medical disorders, 10
Medicine
    for alcoholism, 87–88
    for arthritis, 99
    orthomolecular, 9–10, 15–16,
        37–38, 90
Meganutrient therapy, 16, 38
Megavitamin therapy, 9–10, 16
Memory, 35, 94–95
Mental disorders, 9–10, 16, 22,
    24, 31, 37, 40–41, 67–68

Meprobamate, 83, 89
Mercury, 18, 22, 29, 43, 69
Mercury poisoning, 22, 23
Metabolic-nutritional viewpoint, 103
Metabolism, 10, 65, 72–73
Metallic taste, 35
Metals, 18, 22–24, 100
Migraine, 44
Milbank Memorial Fund, 27
Milk, 46–47, 64, 65, 69, 84, 103
  dolomite in place of, 106
Milk of magnesia, 39
Mineral supplements, 36, 66, 95, 100–101
Mineral therapy, 37
Mineral water, 71
Minerals, 9–10, 18, 34, 58, 105
  cholesterol and, 58
  food processing and, 47
  the heart and, 39, 63–65
  sources of, 71, 112–115
Minnesota Multiphasic Personality Inventory test, 90
Molasses, 75
Molecular biology, 9
Mol-iron, 106
Molybdenum, 17, 21, 106
MSG (monosodium glutamate), 51–52, 64, 101
Morton's Salt Substitute, 39, 64, 106, 117
Mucous membranes, 43
Muscle fatigue, 32
Mustard, 52

National Cancer Foundation, 30, 58
Naturade, 73

Natural foods, 56, 63–64
Nerves, 10, 40–41, 52, 60
Nervous system, 10, 42
Niacin, *see* Vitamin B$_3$
Nightcap, 82
Nitrates, 49–50, 69, 82
Nitrogen dioxide, 43
Noludar, 89
Nucleic acids, 19, 96
Nutmeg, 69
Nutrient therapy, 90–91
Nutrients, 9, 15, 60, 62–68, 73
  adequate supply of, 16
  for atherosclerosis, 96
  in beer and wine, 97
  cooking and, 70
  weight reduction and, 79
Nutrition, 35, 45–47, 54–71, 74, 94–97, 103–107
  alcoholism and, 87, 90–91
  arthritis and, 100–101
  heart disease and, 38, 63–65
  U.S. Senate Committee on, 58
Nutrition Against Disease, 100
Nutritional balance, 5
Nutritional guidance, 103–107
Nutritional therapy, 9–10, 58
Nuts, 64, 68, 76, 100

Oils
  fish liver, 31, 96
  polyunsaturated, 101
  safflower, 77, 101, 103, 106
  salad, 103
  vegetable, 48–50, 65
Onions, 65
Orange juice, 65
Organic foods, 48
Orthomolecular Medical Society, 10, 11

Orthomolecular medicine, 9–10, 15–16, 37–38, 47, 90
Osmond, Dr., 36
Osteoarthritis, 99
Overactive mind, 38
Overweight, 72, 74, 79–80
Oxalic acid, 69
Oxidants, 48
Oxidation, 95
Oysters, 64
Ozone, 43

Pain, 35, 38, 39, 52, 101
Pain killers, 38
Pancreas, 65, 66
Pantothenic acid, 62, 100
Paranoia, 35, 41, 90
Parsley, 65, 70–71
Pauling, Linus, 9, 15, 29, 30
Peaches, 65
Peanuts, 65, 68
Peas, 57, 69, 83
Peppers, 65, 76, 95, 101
Perceptual distortions, 91
Pesticides, 48
Petering, Harold, 58
Phosphate, 64
Phosphorus, 17–18, 42, 62, 71
Physical distress, 10
Physicians, 16, 34–38, 47
Pituitary gland, 42
Placidyl, 89
Plant protein, 61
Plumbing, 37, 96
Poisonous metals, 18, 22–24
Pollution, 37, 43, 69
Polyunsaturated oils, 101
Popcorn, 59
Potassium, 18, 21, 39, 42, 64, 70
    sources of, 21, 70–71, 106, 115, 117

Potatoes, 57, 68, 71
Powdered milk, 103
Preservatives, 48–50, 64
Preventive medicine, 16, 36, 38
Proteins, 56, 60–62, 66, 84, 91, 101
    sources of, 46, 57, 61, 62, 101
Protein diet, 91
Prunes, 64
Psychiatric disorders, 16
    See also Schizophrenia
Psychosis, 35
Psychotherapy, 38
Psychedelic drugs, 69
Psychometric tests, 90
Puberty, 105–106
Public health menaces, 37–44, 85
Pulse, 39
Pumpkin seeds, 68
Pyri-Zinc liquid, 104
Pyridoxine, *see* Vitamin B_6
Pyroluria, 41

Quaalude, 89

Radiation, 69
Radioactive iodine, 43, 69
RDA (Recommended Daily Allowance), 26
Rectum, cancer of, 53
Reducing, 72–80
Refrigeration, 69–70, 47–48, 59
REM (Rapid Eye Movement), 81
Rheumatoid arthritis, 36, 99, 100, 101
Rhubarb leaves, 69
Riboflavin, *see* Vitamin B_2
Rice, 61, 62

Rose-hips, 31
"rum fit," 89

Saccharine, 75
Safflower oil, 77, 101, 103, 106
Salad dressing, 70
Salad oil, 103
Salads, 77
Salt, 53, 105, 106
Salt-free diet, 64
Salt substitute, 39, 64, 70, 77,
    106, 117
"Sara Syndrome," 41
Saturated fats, 53, 57–58, 63, 64,
    97
Schizophrenia, 10, 16, 22, 31,
    40–41, 67–68
Seafood, 68, 100, 101
Seasoning, 70
Seawater, 18
Sedatives, 82, 83
    See also Drugs
Seeds, 60–61, 65, 68
Selenium, 17–18, 20, 29, 64
    sources of, 20, 62, 65, 114
Self-diagnosis, 34
Senility, 15, 94–96
Senior citizens, 97
Serax, 89
Serum copper, 41, 100
Serum hepatitis, 31
7-dehydrocholesterol, 27
    See also Vitamin D
Sex, 79
Simeons diet, 73
Simkin, Peter, 35
Skimmed milk powder, 103
Skin disease, 28, 32, 35, 105
Sleep, 38, 81–84, 88
Sleep-producing drugs, 88

Sleeping pills, 38, 82
Smoking, 44
Sociopathic tendencies, 90
Sodium, 73
Sodium nitrate, 50
Soft drinks, 64, 76
Soft water, 71
Soybeans, 68–69
Spinach, 57, 71
Spinal cord, 60
Sprott, Richard L., 97
Sprouted grains, 60–61
Stanford Medical School, 47
Steroids, 99
Stillman diet, 72–73
Stomach, cancer of, 58
Streptococcus, 100
Stress, 61, 65, 100
    See also Hypertension
Stretch marks, 61
Strokes, 38, 63–65
Strontium 90, 43, 69
Stuttering, 35
Sugar, 37, 42–43, 48, 53, 65–67,
    75, 90
    food sources of, 97
Suicide, 85, 91
Sulfur, 17–18, 101, 113
    sources of, 20, 62, 63, 65, 71
Sunflower seeds, 68
Sweet potatoes, 57, 68
Sweet Tooth Diet, 73
Synthetic emulsifiers, 50–51
Synthetic food colorings, 51
Synthetic foods, 49
Synthetic steroids, 99

Tappel, Aloys L., 95
Tanaka, Yukio, 35
Taste, metallic, 35

Taylor, Keith, 46
Tea, 84
Teenagers, 105–106
Thiamine, *see* Vitamin B₁
Thought disorder, 35
Tin, 17
Tobacco, 44
Tocopherol, *see* Vitamin E
Tomatoes, 96
Tooth decay, 71
Toxic elements, 22–24, 43
Toxicity, 49–50, 95
Toxins, 68–69
Trace elements, 10, 15–25, 42,
    47–48, 63, 91
  sources of, 70–71, 75
Trace minerals, 17–18, 70
Tranquilizers, 38, 82, 88
Tranzene, 89
Trauma, 100
Triclos, 89
Tryptophan, 62, 84
Tumors, 58

Unsaturated fats, 57–58
Uric acid, 73
USRD, 26

Valium, 39, 89
Vanadium, 17–18, 24
Vegan, 60
Vegesalt, 70, 77
Vegetable juices, 70–71
Vegetable oils, 48–50, 65
Vegetables, 68–71, 94, 96, 100,
    101
  cooking of, 70, 117
  food processing and, 47–48
  protein in, 46
  sugar in, 97

Vegetarian diet, 58–62, 74
Vegex, 61–62, 71
Vicon C, 106
Vicon Plus, 105, 106
Vinegar, 70, 73
Vitamin A (carotene), 26–29, 39
  aging and, 95–96
  daily intake of, 106
  food processing and, 47
  for the heart, 43, 64
  for hypoglycemia, 66
  sources of, 28, 62, 65, 96, 108
Vitamin A supplements, 49
Vitamin B complex, 27, 28, 42,
    43, 66, 79, 96
Vitamin B₁ (thiamine), 26, 28,
    108–109
Vitamin B₂ (riboflavin), 26, 28,
    62, 109
Vitamin B₃ (niacin), 16, 27, 28,
    63, 90, 100, 109
Vitamin B₆ (pyridoxine), 18–19,
    27, 38–39, 83–84
  for alcoholism, 90
  for arthritis, 100
  daily intake of, 36, 104–105
  for diet, 73, 79
  dream recall and, 28, 84, 105
  schizophrenia and, 41, 67–68
  skin problems and, 28
  sources of, 48, 62, 68, 110
  weight and, 79
  zinc and, 18–19, 24, 28, 38, 79
Vitamin B₁₂, 28–29, 32–33, 60,
    94–95, 106
  cobalt and, 22
  sources of, 62, 110
Vitamin C (ascorbic acid), 27,
    29–31, 83, 101
  for aging, 94–96
  for alcoholism, 91

as an antitoxin, 43, 95
for arthritis, 31, 101
cholesterol and, 30, 63
copper and, 29, 41
daily intake of, 36, 105
food processing and, 37
for hypoglycemia, 42, 43, 66
kitchen knives and, 70
schizophrenia and, 16, 31
sources of, 31, 65, 94, 95, 110–111
stress and, 38, 39, 61, 65, 95, 100
zinc and, 29
Vitamin D, 27, 29, 43, 60
sources of, 31, 111
Vitamin deficiency, 27
Vitamin E (tocopherol), 27, 31–32, 48
for aging, 32, 95
for alcoholism, 90
as an antioxidant, 32, 95
as an antitoxin, 43
daily intake of, 32, 36, 106
for the heart, 32, 64
for hypertension, 39
as an oxidant, 48
selenium and, 20
skin problems and, 28, 32
sources of, 48, 65, 95, 111
Vitamin F, 27
Vitamin K, 27, 29
Vitamin L₁, 27
Vitamin L₂, 27
Vitamin M, 27
Vitamin P, 27
Vitamin pills, 9
Vitamin supplements, 36, 64, 66, 94–95, 100–101
FDA and, 53
copper in, 104

Vitamin therapy, 37, 83, 90–91
Vitamins, 26–33, 108–112
in cooking water, 70
excess of, 61
food processing and, 47
food sources of, 108–112
glucose metabolism and, 42, 43
the heart and, 63–65
individual needs of, 34
mental disorders and, 9–10
with minerals, 104
trace elements and, 18
water-soluble, 32, 47

Water, 37, 38, 70–71, 76, 104
Water pill, 39
Water pollution, 37, 43
Water-soluble vitamins, 32, 47
Watercress, 69
Weible, Dorothy G., 27
Weight control, 72–80
Weight Watchers, 74
Wheat germ, 48, 59, 64, 65, 83, 103
White flour, 48
White spots on fingernails, 35, 61, 105
Whole grains, 48, 59, 64
Whole wheat, 48
Williams, Roger, 63, 99, 100
Wine, 97
Wynder, Ernst L., 58

Yeast, 90
See also Brewer's yeast
Yoghurt, 59, 69

Zen macrobiotic diet, 73
Zimag C, 106

Ziman Fortified, 100, 105
Zinc, 17–19, 40–41, 48, 68, 96
  for adults, 106
  for aging, 94–96
  for alcoholism, 89, 91
  for arthritis, 36, 100
  blood pressure and, 48
  cadmium and, 23
  for children, 105
  cholesterol and, 39, 58, 63
  copper and, 19, 24, 35, 38, 41
  hypertension and, 38, 39, 48
  for hypoglycemia, 38, 43, 66
  for infants, 104
  manganese and, 38, 41
  schizophrenia and, 10, 41, 67–68
  skin problems and, 28

  sources of, 19, 48, 62, 64–65, 68, 94, 112
  for teenagers, 105
  vitamin B_6 and, 18–19, 24, 28, 38, 79
  vitamin C and, 29
  weight reduction and, 79
Zinc-copper imbalance, 35
Zinc deficiency, 17, 19, 24, 35, 60–61, 89
  arthritis and, 36, 100
  in children, 105
  effects of, 44
  hypertension and, 39
Zinc gluconate, 36, 39, 79, 95, 104
Zinc sulfate, 36
Zinc supplement, 44, 79, 100

🍁 Recipe Index

Almonds, 141

Bananas, 176
Beans, 121, 130, 165
Beef, 127, 148–149
Beef liver Stroganoff, 148
Beef stew, 148–149
Breads, 170–173
Broccoli, 131
Burritos, 154

Cabbage, 132, 133, 166
Cake, carrot, 174
Calf's liver, 146, 147
Carrot cake, 174
Casseroles
  eggplant, 151
  tuna, 137
Cheese, 131, 160–161, 168
Cheese soufflé, 161
Chicken, 139–143
Chowder, clam, 125
Cioppino, 120–121
Clam chowder, 125
Clam sauce, 136–137
Clams, 120–121, 125, 136–137
Cock-a-leekie, 120
Cookies, 176
Corn bread, 172
Corn soufflé, 159

Curried turkey breast, 145
Curried vegetable dish, 153

Desserts, 174–176
Dill sauce, 134–135
Dumplings, 147, 148–149

Eggplant casserole, 151
Eggs, 156–162
Eggs au gratin, 160–161
Eggs Florentine, 160

Fish, 120–121, 134–136, 137

Garlic soup, 123
Gazpacho, 119
Greek marinade, 164–165
Greek salad, 128–129
Greens, 168–169

Herbs, 156, 162
Herring, 134–135

Leeks, 12, 130–131
Lentils, 124, 130–131
Lettuce, 128, 132
Lima beans, 130, 165

189

Linguine, 136–137
Liver, 146–148
Lobster, 120

Mayonnaise, 133
Meat, 146–149
Minestrone, 126–127
Mock veal scallopini, 144
Mushrooms, 135, 139, 152–155, 157
Mushrooms, polonaise, 154–155

Navy bean soup, 121
Normandy salad, 132
Nutburgers, 150–151
Nuts, 141, 175

Oatmeal bread, 171
Oatmeal cookies, 176
Omelets, 156–159
Omelette fines herbes, 156–157
Omelette provençale, 158–159
Onions, 147, 155, 162
Organic salad, 133
Oysters, 122, 134

Parsley dumplings, 147, 148–149
Peanut butter soup, 122–123
Pears, 175
Peas, 123
Piperade, 158
Pot au feu, 127
Potatoes, 163, 167
Poultry, 139–145
Prawns, 138

Red cabbage, 132, 166
Rye bread, 172–173

Salads, 128–133, 136
Sandwiches, 141
Sauces
    clam, 136–137
    dill, 134–135
Seafood, 120–122, 125, 134–138
Sesame, 176
Shrimp, 120–121, 138
Soufflés
    cheese, 161
    corn, 159
    vegetable, 167
Soups, 119–127
Spinach, 129, 160, 164, 168
Spinach timbales, 164
Split pea soup, 123
Stew
    beef, 148–149
    oyster, 122
Stroganoff, beef liver, 148
Sweet potatoes, 167
Sweets, 174–176

Tarts, 155, 175
Tuna fish, 136, 137
Turkey, 143–145

Vegetable burgers, 152
Vegetable curry kinariwala, 153
Vegetables, 124–127, 132, 150–155, 163–169
Vegetable salad, 132
Vegetable soufflé, 167
Vegetable soup, 124–125